Beyond Austerity –
Democratic Alternatives
for Europe

Stuart Holland

SPOKESMAN

First published in 2016 by

Spokesman
Russell House
Bulwell Lane
Nottingham NG6 0BT
England

Phone 0115 9708318
Fax 0115 9420433
www.spokesmanbooks.com

Copyright © Stuart Holland

All rights reserved. No part of this book may be reprinted or reproduced or utilised in any form or by any electronic, mechanical or other means, now known or hereafter invented, including photocopying and recording, or in any information storage or retrieval system, without permission in writing from the publisher.

A catalogue record is available from the British Library.

ISBN 978 0 85124 854 7

Printed in Nottingham by Russell Press (www.russellpress.com)

Contents

Introduction   7

Chapter 1   13
Democracy in Question
   Federal Ambitions and Illusions – Sleepwalking – Confederal Alternatives – Perceptions, Misperceptions and Austerity – Borrowing as Credit and Debt as Guilt – Displacing a Nil Debt Base – Splitting, Denial and Projective Identification – Hegemony by Design, and by Default – Brüning, Austerity and the Rise of Hitler – Weber Misleads on a Protestant Ethic

Chapter 2   42
Learning Up from the New Deal
   Roosevelt and the New Dealers – Contrasts: The New Deal and European Austerity – Similarity: Stalling When Trying to Balance Budgets – Planning as Reinforcing Democracy: The Tennessee Valley Project – Friedmanite Fictions: Denying New Deal Job Creation – Disproving Hayek – Safeguarding Democracy

Chapter 3   54
The Case for a Social Europe
   Delors and After – Gaining Recovery by Eurobonds – Not Counting on National Debt – A European Venture Capital Fund – The Essen Council and Labour Intensive Employment – Commission Displacement and Denial – Mitterrand, Rocard and Recovery – Turning Helmut Kohl

Chapter 4
Regress: From Delors to Juncker   71
   The Feasibility of a European New Deal – Support from European Trades Unions and Employers – False Start for

the Juncker Recovery Agenda – 'Fake Money' – Not Needing New Criteria – Positive Investment Multipliers – Without Needing New Institutions – Recycling Global Surpluses

Chapter 5   89
Beyond a German Europe
Return of 'The German Question' – Schäuble, Syriza and the Denial of Dialogue – Forced Exits? – Marginalising the IMF – Inhibiting the ECB – Compounding Commission Incompetence – The Troika in Question – Neither 'Southern Sinners' nor 'Northern Saints' – Nor Over Merkel's 'Dead Body'

Chapter 6   109
Regaining the Case
Confederalism and the UK Referendum – Iberian Challenge 1: Portugal – Iberian Challenge 2: The Spanish Labyrinth – Restoring Plural Institutional Roles – Political Geometry – Getting it Clear – Mobilising Latent Synergies – The Democracy in Europe Movement DiEM25 – The END European Nuclear Disarmament Precedent

Annex A Modest Proposal for Resolving the Eurozone Crisis   131
Yanis Varoufakis, Stuart Holland and James K. Galbraith
Prologue – The Nature of the Crisis – Four Political Constraints – Four Alternative Policies – Policy 1: A Case-by-Case Bank Resolution Programme – Policy 2: A Limited Debt Conversion Programme – Policy 3: An Investment-Led Recovery and Convergence Programme – Policy 4: An Emergency Social Solidarity Programme – Cutting the Gordian Knot.

Figures

1.1 Jastrow-Wittgenstein and *Gestalt*	22
1.2 Deflation by Decree: Weimar Germany and Troika Greece	33
3.1 An Investment-Led Recovery and a European New Deal	73

Table

2.1 Denial of New Deal Employment Creation	49

Glossary 149

Endorsements of *Europe in Question* 153

Biographical Note 156

Introduction

This book draws on my *Europe in Question – and what to do about it,* published by Spokesman as an eBook in October 2014 and as a paperback in January 2015. Much to most of which has been updated since then including reporting the struggle of Yanis Varoufakis on behalf of Syriza to gain consideration in the Eurogroup of eurozone finance ministers of *The Modest Proposal* by us and James Galbraith.

Some comment in Greece and elsewhere has submitted that he and Syriza were unrealistic in claiming that the EU should consider alternatives to austerity. Yet the force of *The Modest Proposal* is that it sets out means for gaining a recovery of the European economy through bond finance on the lines of the US New Deal, but on a confederal rather than federal basis, without new institutions, without treaty revisions, and without fiscal transfers or financial guarantees from Germany or any other member state.

This so far has been confounded by combination of arrogance, inconsistency and incompetence at the highest levels. The arrogance is that of an increasingly hegemonic Germany, personified by its finance minister Wolfgang Schäuble who, in the Eurogroup of Eurozone finance ministers – which has no basis in any Union Treaty and no rules of procedure – refused to consider the case put by Varoufakis that a recovery for Greece depended on a European recovery. Thus *The Modest Proposal* did not fail. The Eurogroup failed to try it.

The inconsistency is in broken commitments of Commission President Jean-Claude Juncker. In his adoption address to the European Parliament in June 2014 he declared that the top priority for his Presidency would be a €300 billion 'recovery programme' backed by European Investment Bank bonds. By

November he had allowed this to be gelded to €5 billion from the EIB plus recycling of some research funds in what otherwise is a PFI private finance initiative wish-list.

Another broken Juncker commitment to the Parliament was 'Restoration of the Community Method', which means the Commission making proposals to all member states rather than submission to the interests of only one of them. Yet, in dropping his commitment to a major bond backed recovery by the EIB, Juncker had succumbed to the phobia against bonds of Angela Merkel and Wolfgang Schäuble.

This is based not only on prejudice against borrowing, which in the German *Schuld* means both 'debt' and 'guilt', but also on ignorance. Thus Angela Merkel – as in an 'over my dead body' declaration on Eurobonds – wrongly assumes that these must be guaranteed, underwritten and financed by German taxpayers. Whereas EIB bonds since 1958 never have been guaranteed or underwritten by member states.

Angela Merkel also has claimed that you can't solve a national debt crisis by piling on more debt. But EIB borrowing does not count on national debt, even if she is not alone in displacing this. At a meeting in Brussels in December 2014, neither the economic adviser to Council President Donald Tusk nor the advisers to Jyrki Katainen, Commissioner for Investment and Growth, nor to Marianne Thyssen, the Commissioner for Employment, nor the senior economic adviser to the Commission knew this. Whereas, it was immediately confirmed at the meeting by Philippe Maystadt, a former president of the European Investment Bank.

The incompetence of the Juncker Commission also is evidenced by its introducing a European Fund for Strategic Investments – EFSI – on the grounds that the similar sounding

European Investment Fund (EIF), introduced by Jacques Delors, could not do this, rather than offer support for small and medium firms. Which was with reference to the EIF's website rather than a reading of its statutes. The case for the European Investment Fund, which I had made to Delors, was that while the European Investment Bank is project based, the EIF could fulfil a complementary macroeconomic role by recycling global surpluses, which still is credible and illustrated in what follows.

The Commission also has been intent to invent criteria for investments by the unneeded European Fund for Strategic Investment, displacing that these were defined for the European Investment Bank in 1994 by heads of state and government in the European Council as Trans-European Networks – TENS – for both transport and other communications, and extended by them in 1997 to include investments in health, education, urban regeneration – anything in urban societies – and green technology. When I asked a key adviser to Juncker, in March 2015, whether she knew of this, she excused herself on the grounds that 'it was a bit before my time'.

Which is emblematic of the failed legitimacy of the European Commission, which has displaced that European heads of state and government have approved financial institutions that can fund a recovery of the European economy, and employment, without any new institutions or Treaty amendments.

Besides which, if member states invest in the unneeded European Fund for Strategic Investments – EFSI – this will count on national debt under the Excessive Deficit Procedure, whereas Germany and a subservient Commission displace that the European Investment Bank – and its sister institution the European Investment Fund – can finance a European recovery without this doing so. While calling the EFSI a Fund also is a misnomer. With only €5 billion of EIB bond funding, it is not a Fund but an alibi for inaction, and a confirmation of German presumption that debt is guilt, rather than its inverse, credit, implying confidence as well as belief.

Yet such a combination of arrogance and ignorance is increasingly open to challenge by other member governments, including that of Matteo Renzi in Italy, who has compared the failure to address both economic recovery and the refugee crisis to the orchestra on the sinking Titanic.

With a similar rejection of austerity by Antonio Costa in Portugal, who has managed the feat of combining the forces of the social democratic, radical and communist Left in Portugal, and has made a major contribution to the feasibility of a European recovery in claiming that this is more important for survival of the European Union, and for democracy, than leaving decisions to finance ministers in the Eurogroup intimidated by rating agencies.

While also Pablo Iglesias of Podemos in Spain and Sanchez of the PSOE have reason to reject austerity. I am writing this in February 2016, but a Spanish version of my earlier book, *Europe in Question – and what to do about it,* will be published in March. I anticipate meeting them and their advisers in April, as well as scheduled meetings with trades unions and civil society groups in both Barcelona and Madrid.

While also, if belatedly, there is potential joint action with France, when a presidential candidate, François Hollande, was reported as saying that he would follow my advice to issue eurobonds to mutualise debt and launch a European recovery'.[1] On which, as shown in what follows, he tried, but initially in isolation. Yet, thereafter, as President, he declared that he did not believe in a United States of Europe, and that Europe could gain a recovery with the financial instruments it already has, and within existing Treaty provisions, which was well informed.

And also right in that, while much of the debate on Europe assumes that its alternatives are either federalism or nationalism, this neglects that EU governments have the power to govern since they can define 'general economic policies' which besides, through a procedure known as 'enhanced cooperation', need not be unanimous. By such a procedure, a third of member states can adopt a policy without unanimity. Germany cannot object to this in principle, since it has invoked it with 10 other member states for a Financial Transaction Tax in order to outflank David Cameron. He, with others, could invoke it for a European recovery programme to outflank Germany.

In other words, European governments already have the power to govern, rather than rating agencies or Troikas rule. And within a *de facto* confederal framework rather than the rhetoric of commitment to 'ever closer union'.

Which is relevant to a British referendum on EU membership. Reacting to the 3.5 million votes at the last general election for the UK Independence Party, and concerned at a resurgence of the refugee crisis, David Cameron committed himself to negotiate a new settlement for the UK within the European Union. On which expectations among other member states were low. Yet which, in February 2016, substantially succeeded. Not least with explicit reference to the 'enhanced cooperation' procedure by which some member states can adopt a policy without imposing this on others and which, even if few of those agreeing this may have been aware, also compares with Charles De Gaulle's Luxembourg Compromise of January 1966 whereby a member state could decide that a proposed policy was 'not in its national interest' and not adopt it.

Thus, Europe has the institutions and financial instruments to achieve what notably has been missing since the onset of the Eurozone crisis – offsetting deflation by bond funded social investments generating recovery of high levels of employment and mutual trade. Also doing so without relying first on a recovery of private sector confidence, since this would be restored by the multipliers generated by the social investment programme. And thereby to show that it can add value to what national governments otherwise cannot as readily achieve themselves.

Such as that borrowing by its main investment institutions does not count on national debt anymore than US Treasury borrowing, which does not count on the debt of California or Delaware. Yet without needing federalism to achieve this. Which also is relevant to the refugee crisis and the rise of reactionary nationalist parties. Fear and extremism spawn on unemployment. Full employment for Europe, which is feasible, would reduce this. While also needing migrant labour, such as from refugees, to sustain services and other employment in what otherwise is an ageing continent.

Note
1. Euroactiv/france (2011). François Hollande promet de casser certains principes établis. … en suivant un économiste britannique et ancien député travailliste, le bien nommé Stuart Holland. … Le candidat socialiste est favorable aux eurobonds.

Chapter 1
Democracy in Question

Europe was the cradle of democracy. Yet recently has risked being its grave. The sovereignty of Hobbes' *Leviathan* has passed from nation states to financial markets. In responding to a crisis caused by banks, European governments have salvaged them from speculative folly and allowed unelected rating agencies to rule. In an act of mutual self-denial, most of them endorsed a Stability Treaty on financial governance demanded by Germany that can 'compel' them to reduce debt and deficits and commits them to 'balanced budgets',[1] despite this being as regressive a response to crisis as a return to the gold standard.

Some of this was abetted by Milton Friedman claiming that markets are more efficient than governments; that they will maximise social welfare through self-interest countervailed by sovereign consumers; that business has nothing to do with ethics; that its deregulation is the basis of a free society, and alleging support for this both from Adam Smith's metaphor of an invisible hand and Smith's recognition that it is not through benevolence that butchers, brewers or bakers sell us meat, beer or bread.[2]

What emerged was a dominant ideology that only austerity can redeem debt and deficits and a denial of Adam Smith's parallel claim that functional economies depend on functional and just societies.[3] This deepened Europe's long standing democratic deficit. Austerity as faith, as if there were no alternatives, also breached successive European Treaty commitments to rising standards of living and social inclusion, and risked disintegration not only of the postwar 'European project' but also of whole economies and societies.

For the first time since World War Two, the eurozone crisis enabled Germany to achieve a hegemony in Europe that Adenauer, Brandt, Schmidt and Kohl did not want. But this chapter submits that this was not only due to design faults for the euro – though there were – nor due only to rating agencies, but also deeper rooted in both psychology and history. The crisis enabled Germany to displace a darker past and project herself to the rest of Europe as a model of economic, social and political virtue. Besides which, the design faults of the euro also were deeper rooted in a model of supranational decision-making by which a majority of member states could impose decisions on others.

Federal Ambitions and Illusions

In 2004, the American political scientist Jeremy Rifkin published a book called *The European Dream*.[4] Unlike the United States, the European Union appeared to be a model of an emerging 'soft power' in a hard world. Already an economic giant, with a single currency stronger than the dollar, it appeared to lack the earlier arrogance in world affairs of the US. It had emerged from the ashes of World War Two with the ambition for peaceful unification of hitherto warring states. All its members were democracies. With the end of the Cold War, most former satellites of a defunct Soviet Union joined it. Its Charter of Fundamental Rights was to be part of a new Constitution for Europe. It seemed a model for what might in due course be a new global order.

Yet, within months of Rifkin's claims, this proved a delusion. A Constitution for Europe was drafted by a 'Convention' – although appointed rather than elected – chaired by former French President Valéry Giscard d'Estaing, which then was serially rejected by the few electorates given the chance to vote on it. Unlike the US constitution, which was a brief statement of principles, and in the case of a European Constitution could have been one that a European Court of Justice could take into account in judgments to guide, or constrain, governments in European Councils, the Giscard Constitution was a vast compendium of previous Treaties as irrelevant to most people's needs in an already digital age as an out-of-order telephone directory.[5]

The Constitution also failed to highlight that governments could govern for and on behalf of people rather than markets rule. Such as that the requirement to ensure price stability of the European Central Bank was qualified by its parallel obligation, without prejudice to this, to support 'the general economic policies of the Union', which can be defined at any time by the European Councils of heads of state and government. Thus, the statutes of the European Central Bank (ECB) and the European System of Central Banks (ESCB) specify that:

> 'Without prejudice to the objective of price stability, the ESCB shall support the general economic policies in the Union with a view to contributing to the achievement of the objectives of the Union as laid down in Article 3 of the Treaty on European Union.'

While Article 3 specifies that these are:

> 'the sustainable development of Europe based on balanced economic growth and price stability, and a highly competitive social market economy, aiming at full employment and social progress.'

Thus, while aspirations for a federal Europe may in due course be achieved by some member states, although at the risk of others rejecting 'ever closer union', Europe does not need a federal government to resolve its current existential crisis since, with inflation at record lows because of deflation of demand, member states already have the power to define what its key institutions, including the European Central Bank, should do. Which both challenges the myth that it is 'entirely independent' and is more than many national governments can do in relation to their own central banks.

Or, in other words, that the European Union *already has* a government with the additional advantage with regard to those at national level, that its members do not need unanimity to act. Since they can take decisions in terms of 'enhanced cooperation' by which a third or more of them can act on a commmon policy without imposing this on others, i.e. confederal rather than supranational decision-making without implying 'ever closer union', despite the rhetoric concerning this, and which advocates of the UK staying in the EU have neglected.

Which could be invoked for decisions to enable a European recovery, rather than the presumption in particular of one finance minister in one country – Germany – that only austerity will enable recovery, which has failed, failed and failed again, and threatens the destruction of the post-war European project, which had been the aim of such German chancellors as Adenauder, Brandt, Schmidt, and Kohl.

Such as, also, that the European Union already has the financial instruments to ensure its own recovery. As in that bonds issued by the European Investment Bank and borrowing from it do not count on national debt. And that Europe therefore has the equivalent of US Treasury bonds, which do not count on the debt of California or Delaware, without needing a common fiscal policy or fiscal transfers between member states or national guarantees of such borrowing.

The Giscard Constitution, rightly rejected by the few electorates given the chance to vote on it, yet then recycled by governments as a Lisbon Treaty, failed both to highlight this and that, in 1997, governments had given the European Investment Bank – bigger than the World Bank – a cohesion and convergence remit to invest in health, education, urban renewal and environmental protection – the main areas of national public investment. Which aided it in the next decade to quadruple its investment finance to a level four times that of World Bank lending and equivalent to four-fifths of the Commission's budget, but without needing fiscal transfers between member states.

Rather than bringing these investment and job-creating roles of the European Investment Bank 'up front' to parallel its references to the European Central Bank, the Giscard Constitution only cited these facts two hundred pages into its text, in a section headed 'Other Institutions', made no reference to the European Council's 1997 cohesion and convergence remit to it, and simply lifted text concerning the EIB from an annex to the 1957 Rome Treaty, as if nothing had happened since.

Thereby displacing the commitment of the first revision of the Rome Treaty in the Single European Act of 1986 to economic and social cohesion as the 'twin pillar', with the internal market, of the then European Economic Community (EEC). And displacing a 1997 remit to the European Investment Bank to promote economic and social cohesion. Or, in other words, both underinformed and incompetent. Which also has been echoed in the degree to which the key advisers to the Juncker European Commission had no awareness of what heads of government had decided should be the basis of a European recovery programme since 1994, and thought that they had to invent it.

While Juncker then, in 2016, seeking to chastise Matteo Renzi for criticising the Commission, of which more later, entirely neglected that his own Commission was incompetent in proposing a European Fund for Strategic Investments despite the fact that a European Investment Fund, designed to finance an investment led European recovery, had been endorsed by Jacques Delors in 1993 and agreed in 1994 by none less than the Essen European Council.

Which Juncker's own economic adviser, in a meeting with me in March 2015, did not even know. Yet which also entirely contradicts the claim of Wolfgang Schäuble that Greece and other member states 'must obey the rules' since senior officials in the Juncker Commission had no idea of what the 'rules' or guidelines already were, or when they were established by heads of state and government, before Jean-Claude Juncker became its President.

Sleepwalking

Yet such incompetence is not entirely new. The Giscard Constitution was to be agreed as a treaty by heads of state and government. Yet, arguably, it was the worst since the Treaty of Versailles, sharing much with it in the sense in which Keynes had observed of Versailles that:

'it had this air of extraordinary importance and unimportance at the same time. The decisions seemed charged with consequences for the future of humanity; yet the air whispered that the word was not flesh, that it was insignificant, of no effect, dissociated from events.' [6]

The Constitution directly challenged the autonomy of national governments and parliaments by recommending a major extension of Qualified Majority Voting or QMV. In this, 'qualified' does not mean that member states could dissent from it, rather that it was qualified by population, so that the vote of Germany counted more than that of Luxembourg. According to it, and to the earlier 1957 Rome Treaty, such a vote could be carried in a ministerial council if it represented over half of the member states and just under two-thirds of the Union's population.

In principle this meant that member states in such a majority could bind others to adopt a policy irrespective of the intent of their governments, the will of their parliaments, or the wishes of their electorates. It had been in opposition to this that Charles De Gaulle withdrew his ministers from European Councils in mid 1965, and then gained agreement in January 1966 to 'the Luxembourg Compromise', by which Qualified Majority Voting would obtain except in cases of 'important national interest'.

Since any member state could decide what such a national interest was, this, at the time, ground Monnet's supranational design to a halt. But Giscard, who knew this well, nonetheless reinvoked and extended QMV in his draft Constitution. Which risked minoritising and overruling up to half or more of the governments, parliaments and electorates of Europe, unless there were alternative and more confederal decision-making procedures.

Confederal Alternatives

Giuliano Amato, a former prime minister of Italy, who was a vice-president of the Convention drafting the Constitution, realised this risk and proposed such alternative decision-making through Enabling Majority Voting or EMV, whereby a majority vote could allow progress on joint policies by those governments ready to agree them without imposing these on others which either disagreed or were not as yet ready to adopt them.[7] As *de facto* had been the case with the introduction of the euro, which was agreed by some member states yet not imposed on others.

Enabling Majority Voting would have enabled a confederal Europe. But this was rejected out of hand by Giscard. Whereas the projected threat to national democracy in the Constitution, and the principle that national governments and parliaments could be overridden, resonated when the electorates of the few member states to which the Constitution was put for ratification – France, The Netherlands and Ireland – rejected it.

Besides which, Giscard had not even been invited to draft a Constitution for Europe, rather than to outline principles on which it might be based. Unlike Louis XV, who at least saw a storm coming, he saw no impending crisis if national electorates were not to endorse the Constitution. Stendahl deemed that 'style is the man himself' and Giscard embodied elitism, accepting election to the *Immortels* of the *Academie Française* shortly before his all too mortal Constitution was about to be rejected by the only electorates to whom it was put.

After this rejection, in June 2006, Jacques Chirac called for a new European Constitution which would be simpler in form and directly address the twin issues of the democratic deficit and the need for a Social Europe. But governments neither invited him, nor anyone else, such as Giuliano Amato, to redraft a shorter, more succinct constitution more similar to that of the United States. They took out some references such as to a European anthem and recycled it as a Lisbon Treaty which then was endorsed by the Irish electorate – the only one to which it was put – on the basis of an offer it deemed it could not afford to refuse, including a less than thinly veiled threat that, if it were not endorsed, Ireland might be expelled from the Union.

Whereas opinion polls showed that rejecting the Constitution was not because most people at the time were 'against Europe'. For instance, a Gallup poll in France in June 2005 found that 83% of those voting against it thought that 'EU membership is a good thing'; the same share also thought that voting 'No' would give the 'opportunity for a more social Europe' while 80% wanted a treaty that would 'better defend national interests and jobs'.[8]

Perceptions, Misperceptions and Austerity

When the Eurozone crisis hit, this was because rating agencies turned their sights on European governments whose debt, in key cases, had soared to salvage banks from speculation in financial derivatives which the agencies had ranked as safe as government bonds. But the crisis was not caused by the rating agencies. It was a political failure. The agencies had ranked Eurozone national debt at similar and low rates of interest until it became plain that Germany, Austria, The Netherlands and Finland would not support countries such as Greece, Spain, Portugal and Ireland, which were debt distressed after salvaging banks from speculative folly.

The agencies also have been more aware than leading governments that Europe cannot recover from the Eurozone crisis only by cuts and austerity. For example, when Standard and Poor downgraded twelve Eurozone member states' debt in January 2012, it stressed that key reasons were simultaneous debt and spending reductions by governments and households, the weakening thereby of economic growth, and the transparent inability of European policymakers to agree what to do about it.[9]

The political response to the crisis also was a classic case of displacement. The banks had caused it but it was assumed that the public should pay for it. Rather than penalising shareholders, who are supposed to accept losses in the event of failure, governments presumed that public salvage of banks was an unavoidable reality.

Yet what is perceived to be 'for real' depends on the assumptions, presumptions and predispositions of the perceiver. This has been recognised in a wide range of European philosophy and cognitive psychology, even if some of those who claim to lead Europe may be unaware of it.

For example, it was stressed by David Hume, who directly influenced both Adam Smith and also Schopenhauer, who was deeply influential thereafter in both German philosophy and other continental European thought.[10] It then was echoed in the *Gestalt* psychology of Jastrow,[11] the phenomenology of Husserl,[12] and of Merleau-Ponty,[13] as well as by Bourdieu's concept of *habitus* as the environment from which, since childhood, we have consciously or less than consciously acquired the values, beliefs and dispositions that influence our perceptions.[14]

In his *Philosophical Investigations* Wittgenstein drew extensively on *Gestalt*, which in German means form or shape, notably using the Jastrow figure which can be seen as the head of a duck or a rabbit and is reproduced in Figure 1.1.[15]

Figure 1.1
Jastrow-Wittgenstein and *Gestalt*

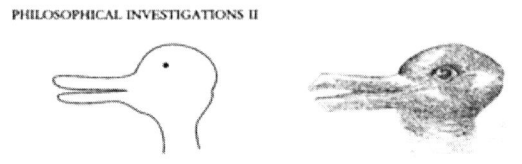

Sources: Wittgenstein, (1953). Jastrow, J. (1899).

The 'fact' of the figure does not change. How we see it can. As significantly, it differs whether one sees it from the right or from the left. From the right it may more clearly be seen as a rabbit; from the left more clearly as a duck. Which may have political parallels in whether one sees borrowing only as debt to be avoided by austerity or its inverse, lending, as credit for investment to lift economies and societies to higher levels of employment, income and wellbeing, as Schumpeter did.[16]

The problems stem from seeing the figure, or an issue, one way only and thereby blocking any alternative perceptions. Such as the perception that there is no alternative to electorates rather than shareholders paying for a banking crisis, or any alternative to reducing debt and deficits to resolve the Eurozone crisis without recognising that the scale of the austerity this imposes risks return to a Hobbesian state of nature.[17] Or in perceiving markets as the highest form of human rationality, rather than seeing them and their imperfections as all too humanly fallible.

Both Freud and Adler drew on Hans Vaihinger who warned against one-way perceptions of what we may presume to be realities, and who submitted that we construct systems of thought, then assume that these match reality and behave *'as if'* the world matches our models.[18] Vaihinger also had observed that, faced with evidence that in principle should make at least some beliefs untenable, they may survive intact as 'practical fictions'.

Which was the case with theories of rational expectations and efficient markets that projected past values on stock markets into future price expectations, and paved the path to the greatest financial and economic disaster for the West since the Wall Street Crash of 1929.[19]

One of the economists most favoured, yet also most misrepresented, by mainstream economic theory, Wilfred

Pareto, had warned against such projection. Thus, in Chapter 1 of his *General Principles of Social Evolution* he allowed that we tend to equate what worked for us in the past with what we expect in future. But stressed that this is different for two main reasons. First, no individual actually can foresee the consequences of a present decision. Second, that:

> '[s]omething that risks being bad in the future is not represented with sufficient intensity in consciousness to balance what may be good in the present'.[20]

Pareto then commented that this can lead to an ungrounded optimism that 'ends by resembling' that of Dr. Pangloss in Voltaire's *Candide*[21]. Voltaire's most famous claim for Pangloss, surveying the ruins of Lisbon after the earthquake of 1755, was his insistence to Candide that he still was convinced that 'all is for the best in the best of all possible worlds', which also was Voltaire's satire on the same claim by Leibniz. Pangloss' perception of the world remained unchanged even when he was hanged, but not dead, due to the incompetence of his executioner, and then subject to a post mortem in which he was still alive.

While the fate of Pangloss has multiple parallels in post mortems for debt-distressed EU member states and their peoples, despite *auto da fé* acts of faith that there is no alternative to cutting debt and deficits on a scale that has denied the commitment of the Rome Treaty to rising standards of living, the commitment of its first revision in the 1986 Single European Act to economic and social cohesion, and serial commitments to solidarity in successive Treaties on the Functioning of the European Union.

Borrowing as Credit and Debt as Guilt

Gestalt perceptions and misperceptions also relate to whether borrowing is perceived as credit, and belief, or as debt and guilt. They also may be less than consciously trapped by language,[22] as with the German and Dutch word for debt – *Schuld* – being the same as for guilt, whereas the inverse perception of borrowing as credit – and belief – has resonance in Latin based languages, and in the Credo of the Creed.

Such a dual meaning of *Schuld* was stressed by Nietzsche in his Genealogy of Morals, in which he also observed that there was a tendency by strong German creditors not only to want repayment from weak debtors, but also to demand penitence for their debt-guilt and to punish them if they did not seek redemption.[23]

The language of redemption also is familiar in relation to bonds, which enable borrowing for a fixed term at a pre-agreed rate of interest with redemption in the sense of lenders then getting their money back if they wish at the expiry of the borrowing term. Most pension funds and sovereign wealth funds balance their portfolios between secure financial investments such as bonds, and the shares or equity of firms which may offer a higher current rate of return, but are more volatile and less secure.

This is standard 'spreading of risk'. Yet, while some bond holders do 'want their money back' at the pre-agreed redemption date, not all do so, rather than seek to reinvest it to continue to earn a fixed interest income. The pragmatic British Treasury until recently has been rolling over bonds which had been issued to finance the Napoleonic Wars and which, without the 'u' in guilt, became known as 'gilts' and thus as good as gold.

Displacing a Nil Debt Base

Yet *Gestalt* in terms of perceptions or misperceptions also is relevant in that while bonds have hit headlines since the

Eurozone crisis, and caused major controversy, much of this has displaced that, until May 2010, when the European Central Bank began some salvage operations for some banks, and then offered them outright monetary support or OMT, the European Union had no debt at all.

Thus, while key member states, as the outcome of salvaging banks, had seen their debt soar since the onset of the Eurozone crisis, the European Union, until mid-2010, had been debt free with a nil debt base, and still in 2016 has a debt level lower than that from which the Roosevelt administration, from 1933, expanded the issue of US Treasury bonds to finance The New Deal.

There is Promethean potential in recognising this, and being unbound from the deflationary debt and deficit conditions required of member states by the 1992 Maastricht Treaty, the later Stability and Growth Pact, which prioritised stability rather than growth, the more restrictive 2012 Stability Treaty demanded by Germany, and competitiveness pacts proposed by Germany in 2013.[24]

By starting from a near nil debt base relative to the United States, the European Union can afford to mutualise a share of the debt of its member states at least up to the 60% national debt limit of the Treaty of Maastricht.[25] Or, alternatively, to mutualise debt over the 60% limit as proposed by Brueghel Institute,[26] and proposed also by the German Federal Council of Economic Advisers.[27] Nor would any of this need new institutions or federalism to do so, rather than political decision within the framework of existing treaties.[28]

Splitting, Denial and Projective Identification

Yet what is blocking feasible alternatives to austerity as a response to the Eurozone crisis is deeper than perceptions of who has what debt and who might be to blame for it. Such as splitting in the sense of denying what is sensed to be bad, and projective identification of what is sensed to be either bad or good onto someone or something else.

Melanie Klein developed these concepts from her studies in child psychology and especially how an infant may projectively identify with a mother's 'good breast' when it is available, yet split from a 'bad breast' when it is denied, and seek to punish the mother by then either refusing to feed further, or to bite it on its return.[29]

Not that Klein was the first or last to analyse displacement and denial. Schopenhauer had done so.[30] Ferenczi had recognised projective identification before Klein,[31] who owed much to him as well as to Freud who had deployed projective identification in his *Totem and Taboo*,[32] which has resonance in totems such as stability and austerity and the taboo of debt and deficits in the Eurozone crisis. His daughter, Anna, recognised both positive and negative projection, as in transference between an analyst and a patient, even if differences between her and Klein, and between American Freudians and British Kleinians, were to be visceral.

Jung,[33] and later Kleinians such as Bion,[34] recognised projection in the sense of externalisation of the self into objects and identification with them, of which the Deutschmark in postwar Germany as a symbol of security has been an example and the Bundesbank its guardian.

Projective identification also has been integral to Germany's role in the Eurozone crisis, and her increasing hegemony, since it has enabled her to escape the legacy of a darker past.[35] As a strong economy when others are weak, she has been able to project herself as a model of economic virtue that should be followed by others.

Thus, mechanisms such as splitting, displacement and projective identification not only are relevant to child psychology.[36] They can also concern individuals, groups, or many or most of those in a society. Dinnerstein has extended Kleinian splitting in terms of splits between heart and head, feeling and reason, private and public and where 'private is deemed good and public bad'.[37] Schneider and Richards have related them to behaviour on markets,[38] of which an example is rating agencies displacing that subprime and other financial derivatives could be toxic and projecting them as safe as government bonds.

Splitting also has been central to the Eurozone crisis in the sense that the increased debt of most EU member states was not due to profligate borrowing other than in one case – Greece – but salvaging banks and hedge funds from their speculation in such financial derivatives. Two of the countries hit hardest by the banking crisis, Spain and Ireland, had much lower levels of debt before the onset of the Eurozone crisis than Germany.

Further, from the onset of the crisis, Angela Merkel sought to deny bonds to mutualise debt in claiming that this would imply a 'transfer union' by which Germany would have to underwrite the debt of other member states. This displaced that Germany need not do so. Issuing them does not imply a fiscal transfer from Germany to other member states any more than the bonds of the European Investment Bank, which has successfully issued them for more than fifty years without a 'transfer union', since EIB bonds are its own liability rather than that of member states.[39]

Her denial also displaced that such mutualisation could be at lower interest rates than debt-distressed governments needed to service their national bonds, reduce deflationary pressures, and release more resources to allow them to import more from Germany.

Part of Angela Merkel's script against issuing Eurobonds has been that you cannot solve a debt crisis by piling on more debt, which is a classic example of Vaihinger's viewing an issue only one way.[40] Adding national debt on debt at 7% or more per year, when growth is low or negative, as was the case in several years during the Eurozone crisis, is suicidal. Issuing Eurobonds for recovery, when interest rates are near or at zero, is not. Eurobonds could recycle global savings through public investments for pension funds and sovereign wealth funds that they cannot currently gain in the private sector,[41] while convincing markets that governments can act to resolve the crisis, for which Standard and Poor called in 2012.

Shifting savings into investments through bonds was how the Roosevelt administration funded the recovery of the US economy from the Depression,[42] while also doing so without major fiscal deficits. Throughout the New Deal until World War Two, these averaged only 3% per year, which was the target level for the Stability and Growth Pact for the euro until Germany, in 2012, demanded that debt-distressed member states balance their budgets through a Stability Treaty.

Besides which, consistent with different *Gestalt* perceptions of the same phenomenon, there are multiple meanings of the word 'bond' ranging from negative implications, as in bondage, through to 'my word is my bond', implying trust, or as a bond implying a reciprocal obligation on lenders and borrowers such as the French or Portuguese for a bond being a obligation – *obligation, obrigação* – between creditors and borrowers rather than implying debt as guilt.

Or as meaning something good, such as bonds being known as *buoni* in Italian, or *boni* in Spanish. Or, in the British case, as already cited, bonds becoming known as *gilts*, and therefore presumed to be 'as good as gold', both before and after Britain was on the gold standard.

Or that a bond can mean bonding together, as in *Bund* in German, and achieve a positive connotation in democratic terms. Such as postwar Germany becoming a *Bundesrepublik* rather than a *Reich*, and redesignating its institutions accordingly, such as a *Bundestag* rather than a *Reichstag*, a *Bundesbank* rather than a *Reichsbank*, a *Bundesbahn* rather than a *Reichsbahn* and a *Bundespost* rather than a *Reichspost*.

While postwar Germany also was committed to bonding with other nations in the construction of a European Union in which, in the words of then French foreign minister, Robert Schuman, would mean that another war between Germany and France not only would be 'morally unthinkable' but also materially impossible. Whereas many Europeans, including many Germans, now see its euro single currency as bondage.[43]

Hegemony by Design, and by Default

A hegemony can be imposed by force, as in Hitler's seizure of power after 1933. Or by Germany imposing it on Vichy France and most of Central and Eastern Europe during World War Two. Or sought by design, as in the earlier aims of the German imperial staff to gain dominance of a *Mitteleuropa*.[44] Yet, as Gramsci allowed, hegemony also may be implicit rather than overt, and passively acquired either by consent, or by default, rather than actively sought by design.[45]

Thus, Germany since reunification has gained a hegemony in Europe that former chancellors such as Konrad Adenauer,

Willy Brandt and Helmut Kohl did not seek, rather than sought to avoid, in part because other member states have allowed it through a combination of financial weakness, since salvaging banks, and fear that, if they defy the emergent economic and political hegemon of a reunified Germany, they will go under. This is despite there being Treaty provisions that could enable a more plural political framework for European recovery rather than debt-guilt presumptions of the need for austerity. As also the political risk for Germany that she is seen by much of the rest of Europe as a malign hegemon.

If, without reference to Gramsci or others on hegemony, some leading German politicians clearly are well aware of this. Thus, the former foreign minister, Joschka Fischer, has claimed that, since Germany twice destroyed Europe in the 20th century, it would be a tragedy if she were to do so again through austerity without, this time, even firing a shot.[46]

In August 2011, Sigmar Gabriel, national chairman of the German SPD Social Democratic Party, and now vice-chancellor of Germany, criticised the 'failed Eurozone crisis management' of the Merkel government for assuming that the problems have been caused by a lack of fiscal discipline by other member states, and argued that only common liability by governments for Eurozone debt could eliminate instability in financial markets. This called for courage, granted that polls of German public opinion by that time showed clear opposition to a 'transfer union'.[47]

The leader of the parliamentary group of the SPD and former German finance minister, Peer Steinbrück, also suggested that Angela Merkel's background in the German Democratic Republic meant she was more distant from the 'European project' than politicians from West Germany, stating that 'until 1989-1990 she had a very different personal and political socialisation than those who experienced European integration since the early 1950s'.[48] Her vehement critics also included Helmut Kohl, who previously had promoted and then been challenged by her, and whom she had replaced as head of the CDU Christian Democratic Union before later becoming Chancellor.[49]

Brüning, Austerity and the Rise of Hitler

Further, one of the reasons why Angela Merkel has gained high support within Germany for opposing joint solutions to the Eurozone crisis, and nearly gained a majority for the CDU-CSU coalition in the September 2013 federal elections, was the wrong presumption that bonds either to mutualise debt or to finance recovery not only would need to be paid for by Germany, but also would risk inflation, and the role that this widely was assumed to have played in Hitler's seizure of power.

Yet this displaces that it was not hyper inflation but deflation and austerity that enabled the rise of Hitler. Until 1929, support for the Nazi Party had not been a threat to democracy. It had not even gained 3% of the popular vote. Hyper inflation in the early 1920s had been a trauma for middle and working classes alike. But had been an outcome of the understandable but counter-productive 'strike' of German capital, in 1922, in response to the occupation of the Rhineland by France under the terms of the Treaty of Versailles. With the closure of firms in its industrial heartland, with little production, lower employment and reduced tax receipts, the Weimar government started printing money which, through 1923, got out of control.[50]

Yet, by the mid 1920s, inflation had been stabilised, not least by the introduction of a new Rentenmark. What later enabled the rise of Hitler was not inflation but deflation. Heinrich Brüning, chancellor from 1930 through 1932, responded to the crash of 1929 by tightening credit and freezing wage and salary increases through an austerity policy which compounded the fall in international demand after 1929, and caused a dramatic increase in unemployment. Brüning also prioritised repayment of reparations under the Versailles Treaty, despite there being no imminent need, since US and other banks already were offering Germany credit without the US making this conditional on such payment of reparations.[51]

It was such austerity that was to prove fatal for democracy in Germany, as it risks being so for Europe now. Brüning lost support with the public, and in the Reichstag, and resorted to government by decree.[52] Within three years, support for Hitler and the Nazis soared from less than 3% to near 44% in 1933, with still rising unemployment, after support for the Nazis had fallen in 1932, when unemployment temporarily fell.[53]

Figure 1.2
Deflation by Decree: Weimar Germany and Troika Greece

Economic performance, 2008/1929=100

GDP figures. Source: Lindner, F. (2013). Greece is like Germany's Weimar Republic. Social Europe, January 18th

Brüning's resort to government by decree since has been paralleled by the decrees of the Troikas of the International

Monetary Fund, the European Commission and European Central Bank since the onset of the Eurozone crisis. Notably, as represented in Figure 1.2, the parallel between what happened in Germany under Brüning and what has been happening since the Eurozone crisis in Greece is striking, yet has been displaced.

Nor has it been widely recognised that the inflation that followed World War Two in Germany was not due to profligate public spending but involuntary scarcity of basic goods and, therefore, inflation in their price. It was only from 1948, with a redistributive currency reform and, through US Marshall Aid, with an investment-led European Recovery Programme rather than Keynesian deficit spending, that the Germany economy began what was to become known as a *Wirtschaftswunder* or economic miracle.[54]

Weber Misleads on a Protestant Ethic

The dual meaning in German – and Dutch – of *Schuld* as both debt and guilt relates also to Max Weber's concept of a Protestant work ethic and widespread misperception that it was this that gave rise to capitalism.[55] Few enough Germans may have read Weber's *Protestant Ethic and the Spirit of Capitalism*.[56] Yet many of them, not without encouragement from tabloids such as *Bild-Zeitung*, know the association of the first two words of its title and contrast this with assumed Catholic or Greek Orthodox self-indulgence.

But Weber's claim that it was a Protestant Ethic that enabled the rise of capitalism was wrong.

Countering him, Richard Tawney showed that this was due to the trading successes of Venice in the Mediterranean and Near East, not least within a Greek Diaspora, and the discovery of the Medici that they could on-lend deposits safeguarded by them for successful Tuscan merchants as credit to others and thereby generate modern banking.[57]

With justification, Tawney claimed that there was plenty of capitalist spirit in Catholic South Germany and among both Protestants and Catholics in Flanders. He submitted that Protestantism adopted the risk-taking, profit-making ethic of capitalism, rather than that capitalism was due to it. Amintore Fanfani has paralleled his criticism of Weber in evidencing that key early Protestant leaders actually *opposed* the credit that was crucial for the rise of capitalism, including both Luther and Calvin.[58]

Thus, Calvin condemned as unlawful any gain obtained at someone else's expense, such as from interest on lending. Through the 16th and 17th centuries, continual prohibitions of usury were issued by the synods of the Protestant French Huguenots and by those of the Dutch Reformers, whose ethical code also condemned excessive labour as diverting time and energy from the service of God.

Jacob Viner, one of the most eminent 20th century economists, also used the example of Scotland to demonstrate that where Calvinism was a state religion, it actually blocked the rise of capitalism.[59] He pointed out that, until well into the 18th century, Scotland was a desperately poor country and that contemporary commentators often remarked on the lack of entrepreneurship and economic initiative from its leaders.

Crowell also has criticised Weber in terms that are consistent with the later Wittgenstein's claims that the meaning of words lies not 'in themselves' but in their context and their use, illustrating that how Weber used the term 'spirit of capitalism' was so arbitrary as to expose him to challenge by a range of critics, asking:

'After all, how is one to define spirit? It is a bit like asking someone to define the word blue. It is up to interpretation, based on context, tone and timing of the use of the word'.[60]

Moreover, there is further relevance now from Weber's misplaced claims for a Protestant Ethic, in that Catholicism allows for a third party intermediation and remission of guilt by a priest, which is similar to the principle of triangulation in group therapy.[61] Whereas both Luther and Calvin stressed that the relationship between man and God was one-to-one, dyadic, direct, and that there was a need to redeem original sin by good works in one's lifetime. While the current German proposals to redeem debt through austerity displaces that it was its inverse – credit – that enabled Europe to emerge from feudalism.[62]

Notes

1. European Council. (2012). Treaty on Stability, Coordination and Governance. Brussels: March. The Treaty reduced the budget deficit level from 3% to 0.7%. It was demanded by Angela Merkel as a condition for, reluctantly, supporting Outright Monetary Transactions by the European Central Bank to protect eurozone countries when they came under attack from financial markets by buying their bonds. In the short term this 'saved the euro'.
2. Friedman, M. (1962). *Capitalism and Freedom.* Chicago: University of Chicago Press. Friedman, M. (1980). *Free to Choose.* New York: Harcourt Brace Jovanovitch.
    Smith, A. (1776). *An Enquiry into the Nature and Causes of the Wealth of Nations. (*Republished 1910). London: Dent.
3. Smith, A. (1759). *The Theory of Moral Sentiments*, Ed D.D. Raphael and A.L. Macfie (1979). Oxford: Oxford University Press.
4. Rifkin, J. (2004). *The European Dream.* New York: Tarcher-Penguin.
5. The European Convention (2004). Proposal for a Treaty Establishing a Constitution for Europe. CONV 850/03 Brussels July 18th.

6. Keynes, J.M. (1922). *The Economic Consequences of the Peace.* London: Macmillan.
7. Holland, S. (2003). *How to Decide on Europe – The Proposal for an Enabling Majority Voting Procedure in the European Constitution.* CEUNEUROP Discussion Paper no. 17. Faculdade de Economia, Universidade de Coimbra. July, 2003.
8. In the Netherlands the proportions among 'no' voters answering the same questions were 78 per cent for Europe as 'a good thing', 71 per cent for 'a more social Treaty' and 73 per cent for a Treaty that would 'better defend national interests'. Manchin, R. (2005). *After the Referenda.* Brussels: Gallup Europe. June 29th.
9. The Telegraph (2012), 'Standard & Poor's cuts ratings of nine Eurozone countries', January 13th.
10. Hume, David (1739, 1740). *A Treatise on Human Nature: Being an Attempt to Introduce the Experimental Method of Reasoning into Moral Subjects.* (1911) Dent, London.
    Schopenhauer, A. (1818). *The World as Will and Representation.* 1st English translation (1883), London: Routledge and Kegan Paul.
    Magee, B. (1997). *The Philosophy of Schopenhauer.* Oxford: The Clarendon Press and New York: Oxford University Press.
11. Jastrow, J. (1899). 'The Mind's Eye'. *Popular Science Monthly*, 54, 299-312. See also Peirce, C.S, and Jastrow, J. (1884). 'On small differences in sensation'. *Memoirs of the National Academy of Science.* 3, 75-83.
12. Husserl, E. (1999). 'Ideas'. In D. Welton, (Ed). *The Essential Husserl: Basic Writings in Transcendental Phenomenology.* Bloomington Indianapolis: Indiana University Press.
13. Merleau-Ponty, M. (1962). *The Phenomenology of Perception.* London: Routledge.
14. Bourdieu, P. (1990). *The Logic of Practice.* Cambridge: Polity Press.
15. Wittgenstein, L. (1953). *Philosophical Investigations.* Oxford: Blackwell.
16. Schumpeter, J. [1911]. (1934). *The Theory of Economic Development.* Cambridge MA: Harvard University Press.
17. Hobbes, T. (1651). *Leviathan: Or the Matter, Forme, and Power of a Common-Wealth Ecclesiasticall and Civill.* Ed. 2nd edition

by I. Shapiro, Yale University Press. 2010.
18. Vaihinger, H. (1912). *Die Philosophie des Als Ob*, or *The Philosophy of 'As If': A System of the Theoretical, Practical and Religious Fictions of Mankind*. First published in English by Routledge and Kegan Paul, 1924. Later republished by Barnes and Noble, New York, 1968.
19. Tett, G. (2009). *Fool's Gold: How Unrestrained Greed Corrupted a Dream, Shattered Global Markets and Unleashed a Catastrophe*. New York: Little, Brown.
20. Pareto, V. (1909). *Les principes générales de l'évolution sociale*, in *Manuel d'économie politique*. Paris: Giard et Brière. 4th edition Geneva and Paris: Droz, 1981. p. 46.
21. Voltaire (1759). *Candide, or the Optimist,* in *Candide and Other Tales*. London: Dent, 1937.
22. Wittgenstein, (1953). Op. cit.
23. Nietzsche, F. (1887). *The Genealogy of Morals*. Translated (1956) by Francis Golffing, Anchor Books.
24. Inversely, for making fire from sparks from Apollo's chariot, Prometheus was bound to a stake and disembowelled, which also has parallels with the fate befalling weak peripheral member states in the Eurozone crisis.
25. Yanis Varoufakis and Stuart Holland (2010). *The Modest Proposal for Resolving the Eurozone Crisis*. yanisvaroufakis.eu/euro-crisis/modest-proposal/
26. Von Weizäcker, J. and Delpla, J. (2010). *The Blue Bond Proposal*, Brueghel Institute Policy Brief, no. 3.
27. GCEE. (2011). German Federal Council of Economic Advisers, November. http://www.sachverstaendigenrat-wirtschaft.de/aktuellesjahrsgutachten.html
28. Amato, G. and Verhofstadt, G. (2011). 'A plan to save the euro, and curb the speculators. The Financial Times International Edition. July 4th.
29. Klein, M. (1932). *The Psycho-Analysis of Children*. London: Hogarth. Klein, M. (1952). *Developments in Psychoanalysis*. London: Hogarth; Klein, M. (1961). Klein, M. (1984). *Narrative of a child analysis*. In R. Money-Kyrle (Ed.). *The Writings of Melanie Klein* (Vol.4). New York: Free Press.
30. Schopenhauer, A. (1818). *The World as Will and Representation*.

31. Ferenczi, S. (1909). *Contributions to Psychoanalysis*. Boston: Badger.
32. Freud, S. (1913). *Totem and Taboo*. London: Hogarth, 1978.
33. Jung, C. G. (1968). *Analytical Psychology: Its Theory and Practice*. New York: Vintage Books.
34. Bion, W. (1962). *Psychoanalytic Study of Thinking*. In *International Journal of Psychoanalysis*. 34: 306-320.
35. Augenstein, D. (2006). 'The reluctance to 'glance in the mirror'. Darker Legacies of Law in Europe Revisited'. *German Law Journal*, 7: 71-82.
36. Sandler, J. (1987). (Ed.). *Projection, Identification, Projective Identification*. London: Karnac.
37. Dinnerstein, D. (1978). *The Rocking of the Cradle and the Ruling of the World*. London: Souvenir Press, p.130.
38. Schneider, M. (1975). *Neurosis and Civilization*. New York: Seabury Press.
    Richards, B. (1989). *Images of Freud: Cultural Responses to Psychoanalysis*. London: Dent
39. See further Holland, S. (2015). *Europe in Question – and what to do about it*. Nottingham: Spokesman Books.
40. Vaihinger, Op. cit.
41. Bain & Company, Global Private Equity Reports, 2012, 2013, 2014.
42. See further *Europe in Question – and what to do about it*.
43. Guérot, U. (2012). *Reinventing Europe: Germany debates political union*. European Council on Foreign Relations. www.ecfr.eu. September 12th. See also Beck, U. (2013). *German Europe*. Cambridge: Polity Press.
44. Fischer, F. (1961). *Griff nach der Weltmacht: Die Kriegzielpolitik des kaiserlichen Deutschland 1914–1918*, i.e. *Bid for World Power: The War Aims of Imperial Germany 1914-1918*. This was translated into English as *Germany's Aims in the First World War*, (1967, NY: Norton and Co.) which displaced that German war aims had been to exploit any provocation for WW1, rather than respond defensively to its outbreak. Which was difficult for German public opinion to accept, although well reported in much of the German press at the time, and confirmed by later research such as Röhl, J. (1994). *The Kaiser and his Court*. Cambridge:

40 *Beyond Austerity*

Cambridge University Press; Von Strandmann, H. P. (1988). 'Germany and the Coming of War', in R. J. W. Evans and H. P. von Strandmann, *The Coming of the First World War*. Oxford: The Clarendon Press; Berghahn, V. R. (1993). *Germany and the Approach of War in 1914*, 2nd ed. Basingstoke: MacMillan.
45. Hoare, Q. and Nowell Smith, G. (1971). *Antonio Gramsci, Selections from the Prison Notebooks*. New York: International Publishers.
  Fusaro, L. (2010). *Gramsci's concept of hegemony at the national and international level*.
  www.iippe.org/wiki/images/…/CONF_IPE_Fusaro
46. Fischer, J. (2012). 'Fischer schlägt Alarm'. *Süddeutsche Zeitung*, June 4th.
47. Spiegel. (2011). *Die Gezeichneten*. September 11th.
48. Euobserver (2013). *IMF urges Germany to show eurozone vision*. August 13th.
49. www.suddeutsche.de/…/euro-krise-kohl-kritisiert-merkel. 17/07/2011.
50. Bullock, A. (1952). *Hitler: A Study in Tyranny*. New York: Knopf.
  Patch, W. (1998), *Heinrich Brüning and the Dissolution of the Weimar Republic*, New York: Cambridge University Press.
51. Schuker, S. A. (1988). *American 'Reparations' to Germany, 1919-1933*. Princeton Studies in International Finance, 61. July.
52. Bullock, A. (1952). Op. cit. Bracher, K. D. (1969). *Die deutsche Diktatur: Entstehung, Struktur, Folgen des Nationalsozialismus*, translated into English as *The German Dictatorship: The Origins, Structure, and Effects of National Socialism*. New York: Praeger 1970.
53. In the election of May 20th 1928 the Nazis gained only 2.6% of the national vote; in that of September 14th 1930 this rose to 18.3%, and by August 31st 1932 to: 37.3%. With a fall in unemployment this had dropped significantly to 33.1% in the election of November 6th 1932. Yet in the election of March 5th 1933, with unemployment again rising, their share of the vote rose to 43.9% and 288 seats in the Reichstag out of a total of 647.
54. Shonfield, Andrew (1965). *Modern Capitalism: the Changing*

Balance of Public and Private Power. London: RIIA and Oxford University Press.

55. As with *Schuld* as meaning both debt and guilt, there is an issue in German in that *Gift*, does not mean giving as in the gift of life, or giving as gaining, as analysed later, but poison and death. My colleague Gerald Wooster has found a remarkable resistance to recognising the significance of this from some German psychologists who insist that the distinction of the words in their different contexts is entirely clear and well understood by Germans, or Austrians. But which implies that there are no unconscious resonances in their meaning which, for a psychologist, whether Freudian, Jungian, Adlerian, Kleinian or otherwise, is less than convincing.
56. Weber, M. (1905). *The Protestant Ethic and the Spirit of Capitalism*, republished in *The Protestant Ethic and Other Writings*. New York: Penguin, 2002.
57. Tawney, R. H. (1926). *Religion and the Rise of Capitalism.* New York: Harcourt Brace.
58. Fanfani, A. (2009). *Catholicism, Protestantism, and Capitalism.* Rome: IHS Press.
59. Viner, J. (1978). *Religious Thought and Economic Society.* Durham: Duke University Press.
60. Crowell, E. (2006). *Weber's 'Protestant Ethic' and his critics.* MA Thesis: The University of Texas at Arlington, p.8. Wittgenstein, L. (1953). Op. cit.
61. Mahler, M. S. (1967). 'On Human Symbiosis and the Vicissitudes of Individuation'. *Journal of the American Psychoanalytical Association* 15: pp740-763.
62. On this point see also Mason, P. (2015). *PostCapitalism. A Guide to Our Future.* Allen Lane, Penguin and Random House UK.

Chapter 2

Learning Up from the New Deal

The 1930s US New Deal was controversial among the advocates of 'sound money policy'. But not among the millions of people it got back into work. This chapter touches on some echoes of controversy concerning the New Deal, but otherwise contrasts its remarkable achievements with the outstanding failure of austerity as a response to the Eurozone crisis.

The New Deal depended especially on Roosevelt's perception as a patrician that his own class was failing not only itself, but also America. His aim was not to preserve a financial oligarchy since he was not convinced that it had justified its privilege by fostering the speculation that led to the Crash of 1929. Like Henry Ford, he was offended that high finance was not concerned to address or resolve the problems of 'the common man' and his family.[1]

The chapter recognises that the United States at the time of the New Deal already was a federal state, with a federal fiscal policy and able to make the fiscal transfers between its member states that are argued by many as the only alternative to the Eurozone crisis. Yet does so also in the context of *The Modest Proposal* that what the New Deal achieved within a federal framework can now be achieved in Europe without 'waiting for federalism'.

Roosevelt and the New Dealers

Roosevelt was not a theoretician but a pragmatist. He told the American public that he would try anything to see if it worked, and if it did not, try something else. But he was trying when the rest of the American establishment – like much of it in Europe now – had no idea of how to gain recovery from the Depression, and he succeeded despite opposition from its Supreme Court, which for some time stalled him.

He was not a Keynesian in the sense of favouring deficit spending. Not only since Keynes did not publish his *General Theory* until three years after Roosevelt first was elected President. He had been under pressure from many of those who supported, and financed, his presidential campaign to balance the budget, and began the New Deal with a reduction of spending.[2]

But this was not for long. A key role in this change was played by the only woman in his cabinet, Frances Perkins, who, independently of Keynes, had grasped that public works would 'pump prime' demand that could recover the economy.[3]

Moreover, as Schlesinger has observed, many of the New Dealers including lawyers, economists, college professors, social workers, and those with experience of city government, like Roosevelt himself, as Mayor of New York, had cut their political teeth at municipal rather than federal levels in trying to improve local economies and societies by whatever means they could devise. They also were open-minded in a manner which shames many leaders of institutions in Europe now. As Schlesinger has put it:

'They were all at home in the world of ideas… They were accustomed to analysis and dialectic; and they were prepared to use intelligence as an instrument of government'.[4]

Some key figures among initial supporters then dissented from what transpired, and resigned.[5] But at a time when American democracy appeared to have lost its way, and people came second to monetary stability, FDR put people first, and showed that government could create jobs and welfare by shifting savings – high in a sustained recession or depression – into job-creating social and environmental investments.

Contrasts: The New Deal and European Austerity

Contrasts between the US New Deal and the lack of one for Europe are under-recognised, less in the sense of denial than mere displacement. Some of those in government in Europe doubtless are aware of Marshall Aid. But fewer of them may have grasped that this was a European recovery programme sanctioned by both Harry Truman and Congress, not only because of the onset of the Cold War but also by the success of the New Deal.[6] From which much could be learned up now.

- Rather than waiting for years to propose a Banking Union which might or might not gain greater regulation of banks, the Glass-Steagall US Emergency Banking Act of 1933 required a separation of commercial banking from speculative investment banking and also insured people's bank deposits.

- Rather than the ECB offering money to banks at 1% or less, which they then on-lend at seven times or more as much to recapitalise themselves, the Reconstruction Finance Corporation lent money to firms which were in debt and threatened with closure, and to others that wanted to invest.

- Rather than waiting for a recovery of private sector investment, the National Industrial Recovery Act of 1933 enabled the US to directly undertake public investment projects.

- Rather than allowing youth unemployment to rise over 50%,

as in Spain and Greece since the Eurozone crisis, it took only 37 days for Roosevelt, from his inauguration on 4 March 1933, to set up the Civilian Conservation Corps (CCC) programme which employed some 3 million men for at least six months, from 1933 to 1941.[7]

- Rather than urging or insisting that southern Europeans should work harder and longer on the lines of a Protestant Ethic, the codes of the National Recovery Administration set limits for working time and minimum wages per hour. 16 million workers were covered by these codes. An 8 hour day and a minimum wage of $1.25 were introduced. A board was set up to investigate and fine those employers who disregarded this.

- Rather than the EU Commission's ritual claim of the need for 'structural reforms', implying reduction of trades union rights, the Wagner National Labour Relations Act of 1935 reinforced them by giving workers the right to form and join trade unions and obliged employers both to recognise them and to take part in collective bargaining. This embodied both a social right and had the explicit aim of increasing wages to increase demand.

- Rather than claiming the need to extend the age for retirement, as some governments in Europe have done since the onset of the Eurozone crisis, or that pensions should be cut, the New Deal 1935 Social Security Act set up the first nation-wide pensions scheme. Workers and employers had to pay into a federal pension fund. Each state was also expected to work out a plan for unemployment insurance. The Act covered and was to benefit 35 million people.

- Rather than alleging that combating poverty was up to EU member states themselves, and refusing to lend funds directly to them, the Reconstruction Finance Corporation lent money to state and local governments to do so.

- Rather than claiming that southern Europe should resolve its own financial crisis, the 1933 Tennessee Valley Development Act and Tennessee Valley Authority administering it included seven of the least developed American states in its Deep South with regional, environmental and social programmes which involved and reinforced the development of local communities.

- Rather than cutting public investment programmes on the spurious claim that this would render peripheral European economies more competitive, the Works Progress Administration (WPA) from 1935 funded the federal highway programmes, built bridges, airfields and post offices; and extended electrical power to rural areas. Over its seven-year history, the WPA alone employed about 8.5 million Americans. With their direct and indirect dependents, it is estimated that some 24 million Americans gained from the WPA.[8]

- Rather than encouraging the rise of an anti-democratic fascist movement, as had been the case in the response of Brüning to the impact of the 1929 Crash in Germany, and now is the case in which it was found in 2013 that 46% of those polled in France supported Marine le Pen and the French neo-fascist National Front, Roosevelt's New Deal regained confidence in democracy.[9]

Similarity: Stalling When Trying to Balance Budgets

Yet, after initial dramatic success, not least in its first 'hundred days', the New Deal stalled in 1937, since Roosevelt temporarily gave way to pressures to balance the budget. The

American economy turned downwards for 13 months through most of 1938. Industrial production declined by almost 30% and production of durable goods fell even faster.

Manufacturing output fell by nearly two-fifths and regressed to 1934 levels. Producers reduced their investments in durable goods, and inventories declined, even if personal income was only 15% lower than it had been at the peak in 1937.

This was among the reasons why full employment for America only came with the World War Two war economy. Yet, what prevented the recession being deeper were the earlier provisions for minimal wages and limits to hours worked. In most sectors, hourly earnings continued to rise, which partly compensated for the reduction in the number of hours worked for those who still had jobs. But, as unemployment rose, consumers' expenditures declined, thereby leading to further cutbacks in production.

None the less, again, and unlike the European Union since the onset of the Eurozone crisis, Roosevelt rapidly learned up. In April 1938, he proposed a further large-scale investment programme to Congress, and gained $3.75 billion, or nearly double private sector investment in 1933, to fund it. Other appropriations raised the total to $5 billion, after which, with positive multipliers generating not only consumer demand but also investment supply from the private sector, the economy recovered.

Planning as Reinforcing Democracy: The Tennessee Valley Project

It also has tended to be overlooked that planning, which had been Marjolin's ambition, in the 1960s, for a Medium-Term Economic Policy Committee, and for key US states in major infrastructure projects after Independence, was integral to the design of the Tennessee Valley Authority. This was approved by Congress in May 1933, following a long period of pressure for the privatisation of government owned properties at Muscle Shoals, Alabama. As Roosevelt put it:

> 'It is clear that the Muscle Shoals development is but a small part of the potential public usefulness of the entire Tennessee River. Such use, if envisioned in its entirety, leads logically to national planning for a complete river watershed involving many States and the future lives and welfare of millions'.[10]

In citing this in his *TVA and the Grass Roots*, Selznick submitted that the TVA also was a social instrument not only *within* a democracy but also reinforcing it at local levels, including the engagement of local communities in their own future, such as in promoting and supporting cooperatives. Selznick then extended this case in terms which are highly relevant to a European Union that has enlarged its market without deepening economic and social cohesion, and risks a centralised bureaucracy as a response to the Eurozone crisis that could further deny the autonomy of elected governments. As he put it:

> 'Centralization has been proceeding apace in all fields of human organization. Efficiency has been, in this view, a rigorous leveller, erasing the diversity of individual enterprise and local control in the interests of large hierarchized unit. … In exchange for the benefits of order and coordination, initiative has been stifled and the power of decision, indispensable element of democratic action, lodged in far-off places, remote from the beneficial influences of local areas which become merely the objects of bureaucratic manipulation'.[11]

In a manner resonant for the crisis now facing small and medium firms in Europe, and also small and medium nation states, he then added that:

> 'Small businessmen, the independent artisan, and farmer alike,

have felt the enervating effect of the concentration of economic and social control. By a similar logic, small nations, too, have been unable to endure alone, and have reluctantly found their way into some broader hegemony which provides security in exchange for liberty'.[12]

Friedmanite Fictions: Denying New Deal Job Creation

The New Deal did not achieve full employment. Only armaments production for and during World War Two did so. Yet what it did achieve in terms of job creation has been subject to claims by some economists that it prolonged the Depression by seven years.[13]

Table 2.1 Denial of New Deal Employment Creation

Unemployment	1933	1934	1935	1936	1937	1938	1939	1940	1941
Counting workers in job creation programmes as unemployed	24.9%	21.7%	20.1%	16.9%	14.3%	19.0%	17.2%	14.6%	9.9%
Counting workers in job creation programmes as employed	20.6%	16.0%	14.2%	9.9%	9.1%	12.5%	11.3%	9.5%	8.0%

Source: Smiley, G. (1983), Recent Unemployment Rate Estimates for the 1920s and 1930s, *Journal of Economic History* 43:2 487–93.

Part of this, as summarised in Table 2.1 by Smiley, who does not endorse the case, was the Friedmanite presumption that jobs created by public works were not 'real jobs'. In a combination of displacement and denial, and Vaihinger's one-way only view of the world, this reflected the case of Milton Friedman that real jobs are created only by markets, not by governments. As Darby has submitted, this 'mislaid' at least three and a half million of them.[14]

Disproving Hayek

Crucially, however, the main finance for the New Deal was not through deficit financing but by shifting savings into investments through an expansion of US Treasury Bonds. Budget deficits from 1933 through to the onset of World War Two averaged only 3% of gross domestic product.

This has significant implications for Europe now. For 3% was the target level for deficits in the EU Stability and Growth Pact, until most member states in the Eurozone engaged in mutual self-denial under pressure from Germany, in 2012, for a Stability Pact and commitment to what amounted to close-to-nil budget deficits.[15]

Not least, the New Deal repudiated the case of Hayek that government intervention and planning is the road to serfdom since it reinforced faith in democracy in the US, evidenced in Roosevelt's serial re-elections. Hayek's case, still influential in Germany, also is a classic example of displacement since, by the time that *The Road to Serfdom* was published in English in 1944, it should have been clear to him that government intervention in the New Deal had reinforced rather than destroyed American democracy.[16]

Safeguarding Democracy

The New Deal also safeguarded the restoration of democracy in continental Europe after World War Two by inspiring the 1948 Marshall Plan, whose 'benign' hegemony contrasted entirely with the authoritarian policies of the Troika in the Eurozone crisis.

First, because the US did not directly manage it rather than devolve its administration to the Organization for European Economic Cooperation (OEEC) headed by Robert Marjolin, a committed Keynesian, who had been deputy to Jean Monnet at the first French Plan.

Second, because it did not simply rely on market forces. Marjolin insisted that the beneficiary member states from Marshall Aid should plan their investment-led recovery. He sent back Italy's first submission on the grounds that he wanted a development plan for the country rather than a 'shopping list for reconstruction'.[17]

Third, since it entailed no 'structural reforms' but, rather, welcomed trades union rights not only since the Roosevelt administration, in the New Deal, had recognised the need for wage demand to promote recovery, and reinforced the rights of trades unions, but also since the US recognised that breaking trades unions had been integral to how fascism in Italy and Germany had been able to overthrow democracy.

Fourth, since Marshall Aid was followed in 1953 by the cancellation of 48% of German debt, i.e. the major debt relief which Germany has denied to debt-distressed Eurozone economies.

Fifth, since, also, Marshall Aid was grant – rather than loan – funded, and based on credit rather than presuming that debt is guilt. It was such grants that enabled German banks to issue counterpart credit in local currency to cash-starved German firms. Combined with the psychological effect of Marshall Aid showing commitment to German recovery by the US, it was the allocation of credit through such counterpart credit by the publicly owned non-profit *Kreditanstalt für Wiederaufbau*, or Credit Reconstruction Institute, that enabled postwar German recovery and encouraged its people to gain confidence in its newly recovered democracy.

Notes

1. Lacey, R. (1987). *Ford: The Men and the Machine*. Op cit.
2. Cohen, A. (2009). *Nothing to Fear*. New York: The Penguin Press.
3. Cit. Cohen, ibid.
4. Schlesinger, Arthur M., Jr. (1958). *The Age of Roosevelt: The Coming of the New Deal*. Boston: Houghton Mifflin, p. 18.
5. Including Raymond Moley, a key figure in the early days of the New Deal, and who later renounced much of it. C.f. Moley, R. (1939). *After Seven Years*. New York: Harper & Brothers.
6. There are several historical records citing this. But my own awareness of it was raised by a one-to-one meeting with Truman in May 1960 at Independence Missouri, where he stressed this when I was visiting scholar at the University of Missouri Kansas City.
7. The CCC improved millions of acres of federal and state lands, as well as creating parks. Recruits planted trees, built wildlife shelters, stocked rivers and lakes with fish, cleared beaches and created camp grounds. New roads were built, telephone lines strung, and some 3 billion trees planted which was crucial in countering the earlier Dust Bowls by retaining water and holding soil in place. Youth crime during the period fell by over half.
8. Although challenged by the US Supreme Court, as were several measures of the first 'hundred days' of the New Deal, the Works Progress Administration of 1935 invested over $10.5 billion and employed 8.5 million workers from 1935 to 1941. It built 77,000 bridges, 664,000 miles of roads, 285 airports, 122,000 public buildings including hospitals and 11,000 schools as well as dams, reservoirs and water control and irrigation systems.
9. Open Europe, 17 October 2013
10. Roosevelt, cit. Selznick, Philip. (1949). *The TVA and the Grassroots: A Study in the Sociology of Formal Organization*. Berkeley: University of California Press.
11. Selznick, ibid., p. 22.
12. Selznick, ibid.
13. E.g. UCLA, Edu. (2004).' FDR's Policies Prolonged Depression by 7 Years'. *UCLA Economists Calculate*, October 8th.
14. Darby, M. R. (1976). 'Three-And-A-Half Million U.S.

Employees Have Been Mislaid: Or, an Explanation of Unemployment, 1934–1941'. *Journal of Political Economy* (1976) 84:1, 1–16,
15. EU (2012). *Treaty on Stability, Coordination and Governance.* Op. cit.
16. Hayek, F. von. (1944). *The Road to Serfdom.* New York: Routledge.
17. Marjolin to the author in 1966.

Chapter 3

The Case for a Social Europe

When Robert Schuman declared, in May 1950, that a European Coal and Steel Community would mean that a further war between Germany and France not only would be morally unthinkable but also materially imposssible, this was well intentioned but, at the time, irrelevant and also unfounded. For by then, hostilities between Germany and France were not credible, whereas a transition from cold to actual war between NATO and the Soviet Union was in the minds of policy makers after Stalin's 1948 blockade of Berlin.

Besides which, Schuman's declaration was unrealistic. Armaments may depend on steel, and fuel, such as – in that era – coal, and therefore energy. But there had been an agreement between France and Germany on energy sharing at the time that Hitler launched the 1939 assault on France through the Ardennes that did nothing to deter it. When Guderian's tanks and German artillery destroyed local power stations, there was an agreement that if there was a power loss between them and those in Germany, it would be restored. Which it was, without deterring the Ardennes offensive.

While also, the aim of the postwar European project not only was to create a common market for coal and steel, which hardly motivated anyone, but also to assure both a democratic and social Europe. On which the key architect, if sharing this ambition with Schuman, was to be Jacques Delors, with values that ranged deeper and wider than only the creation of a common market.

Delors and After

Delors was the longest serving and highest profile president of the European Commission. But although achieving high office he lacked the insider advantages of those who had done so by gaining entrance to the *École Nationale d'Administration*. His advancement had been by and within the CFDT trades union. To his credit he never forgot this, which also is one of the reasons why he opened the space for new initiatives for social dialogue.[1]

Yet, after his then becoming finance minister in the first Mitterrand government, and within three years of his becoming President of the Commission, none of his case for a Social Europe was making progress. One of Max Weber's archetypes of power is charismatic leadership, and Delors had charisma. But he could not get the Weberian bureaucracy of the Commission to design strategies for economic and social cohesion. As I learned directly from him in an early evening one-to-one meeting on 23 March 1988, in an encounter that influenced my deciding to resign from Westminster to help him shape policies and institutions that could do so.

At the meeting he appealed for help. Everyone had heard of 1992 as the date to complete the single market, but where were the policies to realise cohesion as the 'twin pillar' of the 1986 Single European Act? Where was the case for a Social Europe? Where had I been? Why had I been out of touch?

I replied that I had been shadow minister for international development and been all over the world, not least leading the first Labour Party delegation to China since Clement Attlee in 1952. Yet, in any event, I was but an opposition spokesman in one parliament in one country, whereas he not only was President of the Commission but also most of the public thought he already was President of Europe. Surely he had the authority to get new policies through, and had some good people who could help realise the cohesion agenda of the Single European Act? His reply was striking:

'Half the people in this building[2] are here because their governments don't want them. Of the rest, of course, one or two per cent are really good, but they are wholly proccupied in trying to achieve what we decided yesterday rather than thinking for tomorrow. Besides, even the best among them know only of politics in this institution and their own capitals. None of them are thinking long-term as *Out of Crisis* did.'[3]

He also lamented that the only way that even progressive Commission officials could think of cohesion was in terms of reducing regional disparities rather than conceptualising a framework for a Social Europe with both these and structural, social and macroeconomic policies for full employment.

Which emerged at a meeting of a working group that I then chaired at the European University Institute in Florence, where a senior official from the Directorate General for Research interrupted the discussion and asserted that cohesion was only about reducing regional disparities and that the working group should not concern itself with anything else. I told him that if he had nothing better to offer to the discussion he should get the next flight back to Brussels. Which he did, though also later claiming that he would ensure that my report on economic and social cohesion never would get through to Delors, on which he was mistaken.[4]

In the earlier meeting with Delors I said that if I undertook such a report I would need open ended terms of reference and that if I found current thinking unfounded, as with the then Cecchini report which stressed gains from economies of scale in the single market,[5] I would of course say so. He replied that he expected nothing less. In my later interim and final reports to him I stressed that the Cecchini report was misguided since highly competitive companies at the time, such as in Japan, were so not only due to economies of scale, stressed *ad infinitum* by Cecchini, but also economies of scope and continuous improvement – *kaizen* – based on both commitment for core workers to 'lifetime employment' and to profit sharing.[6]

Gaining Recovery by Eurobonds

Delors has been criticised for supporting a single currency without being aware that the national debt and deficit criteria of Maastricht for a single currency risked being profoundly deflationary.

Yet he was well aware that, if there was to be a Social Europe with commitment to high levels of employment and the rising living standards that had been premised in the Rome Treaty, the Maastricht debt and deficit criteria needed to be offset by European policies and instruments to countervail this. Which could not simply be Keynesian in the sense of deficit spending, but needed the bond finance that had funded recovery from the post 1929 Depression in the Roosevelt New Deal.

The final 1993 report on cohesion that I prepared for Delors,[7] with the help of some twenty economists and political theorists from fifteen European countries, was the basis of the target of creating 15 million jobs in his December 1993 White Paper *Growth, Competitiveness, Employment*.[8]

This would have been equivalent at the time to full employment. The econometrics showed that a third of these could be from social and environmental investments; a third by a reduction of working time as a European citizenship right, and a third by more labour intensive employment in the social sphere, i.e. more teachers and smaller classes, more health workers and shorter waiting lists, and more care for the elderly in an increasingly ageing population.

The White Paper was the first time that Europe had set job creation targets rather than only 'create the conditions' for markets to deliver the rising standards of living, which had been one of the first commitments of the Rome Treaty. Its agenda gained considerable attention from the international press, and was seen by Delors himself as the 'high point' of his Presidency.[9]

A key proposal in the cohesion report to Delors was that the Commission should countervail the limits to its 'own resources' and the deflationary implications of the Maastricht debt and deficit criteria for a single currency by the issue of bonds through a European Investment Fund. This was the first statement of the case for what later became known as Eurobonds.

The principle was that, like US Treasury bonds, which had financed the 1930s New Deal and did not count on the debt of member states of the American Union such as California or Delaware, European bonds need not count on the debt of EU member states.

While also, whereas the US was a fiscal union, such bonds issued by a European Investment Fund could be serviced by member states from revenues on the projects they financed, which could be funded by national fiscal receipts which would increase with direct and indirect taxation of the revenues and employment that its investment projects generated.

The projects themselves should parallel those of the US New Deal, in urban regeneration, safeguarding the environment, as well as in health and education. Not least, the European Union at the time – and until May 2010 – had no debt. In borrowing to invest in a European New Deal the European Union would have a late starter advantage relative to the United States.

Not Counting on National Debt

A senior director of the European Investment Bank, Tom

Barrett, then rang me in London to say that he had read my November 1993 report to Delors and Delors' December 1993 White Paper and that Delors, as President of the European Commission, could, of course, gain a new financial institution whose borrowing would not count on national debt if he could persuade the European Council to endorse it.

But Barrett then added that perhaps neither of us realised that of the then EU member states, only two – the UK and The Netherlands – counted borrowings from the European Investment Bank against their national debt, and that whether or not they chose to do so was up to them, and not bound by any Treaty provision.

Barrett's revelation clearly was a move by the European Investment Bank to avoid a rival bond-issuing institution. Yet this was like finding gold without the need for it to back a European currency or a European recovery. Not because the Bank hitherto disguised the point. But it did not advertise that member states either did not, or need not, count borrowing from it on national debt.

Moreover, as I later found, several finance ministers did not know that borrowing from the EIB either did not, or need not, do so. Central bank governors knew, but had no vested interest in volunteering this to a finance minister when, aware of the Maastricht debt and deficit criteria, they were concerned to restrain public spending.

The Essen European Council, following the 1993 cohesion report to Delors, none the less supported its proposal for a European Investment Fund and its key design aims – that it could issue bonds. It was established in 1994.

Yet, although the Fund was set up, and although its statutes then, as now, allow it to issue bonds, its strategic aim for them to fund a broad range of social investments to countervail the deflationary debt and debt conditions for a single currency of the Maastricht Treaty was displaced by opposition from the Directorate General for Economy and Finance of the Commission and the Bundesbank, and went by default.

There therefore was no European Recovery Programme from 1994 to countervail the deflationary Maastricht debt and deficit conditions for a single currency. Austerity reigned and the path thereby opened for it, from the onset of the Eurozone crisis, to rule.

A European Venture Capital Fund

The competitiveness recommendations in the 1993 cohesion report to Delors were that a European Investment Fund should finance an EU-wide venture capital fund from its bond issues for small and medium firms.

The European Investment Fund, set up in 1994, had next to no experience of evaluating the viability of the small and medium firms that might apply for equity finance from it. Yet its design aim was that it should relate to and network with financial intermediaries such as the *Caisse des Depôts et Consignations* in France, the *Cassa Depositi e Prestiti* in Italy, and the *Kreditanstalt für Wiederaufbau* in Germany, as well as regional development agencies which could advise on the risk potential of the applying firms.

But, though stressed in the 1993 cohesion report to Delors, this was displaced in favour of offering only equity guarantees – rather than actual equity – through mainly private sector intermediaries in member states who packaged them with their own interest-bearing loans which could deter new high tech start ups. The difference was crucial. The take-up was minimal, at less then 1 billion ECU over the next five years, rather than the 60 billion which had been part of my design aim for the Fund.[10]

Further, what one of the Commission's other most powerful directorates general, for Transport, wanted to prioritise at the time was not social investments, but Trans-European Networks in rail and communications, for which the lobby pressure in Brussels was significant.

The difference was crucial. High speed transport networks benefit those travellers who can afford their fares, not least when written off as a business cost against tax. Funding much wider social investments in health, education, urban regeneration, safeguarding the environment, with these not counting on national debt, would advantage every citizen, and child, in Europe. While financing a European Venture Capital Fund for small and medium firms and high tech start-ups – and thus equity– could have released them from the strangulating noose of interest-bearing loans which, too often, has meant a high rate of infant mortality in the years before such firms can secure markets. And thus, also, by favouring new high tech start-ups, raise the rate of European innovation.

The Essen Council and Labour Intensive Employment

The case also made in the 1993 cohesion report to Delors that Europe can afford labour intensive employment in the social domains of health, education, urban renewal and social services was not only that this would improve their quality. It also was that such services, as with local protection of the environment, are not subject to global competition in the sense of manufacturing or financial services.

And this, at the time, gained traction. Since, while much of the design for the Delors 1993 White Paper, such as for EU bonds, went by default, he managed to get the principle of labour intensive employment in such social and local services, and environmental protection, endorsed by the Essen European Council the following year. Thus the Essen Presidency Conclusions prioritised:

> 'continuing and strengthening the strategy of the White Paper in order to consolidate growth, improve the competitiveness of the European economy and the quality of the environment in the European Union and – given the still intolerably high level of unemployment – create more jobs for our citizens'.

This also endorsed the case in the cohesion report to Delors for more labour intensive employment in calling for:

> 'increasing the employment-intensiveness of growth, in particular by more flexible organisation of work in a way which fulfils the wishes of employees and the requirements of competition (and) the promotion of initiatives, particularly at regional and local level, that create jobs which take account of new requirements, for example, in the environmental and social-services spheres'.[11]

Yet, since neither the White Paper nor the Essen European Council Conclusions had made the case that governments could shift their national borrowing for social and environmental investments to European bonds without these counting on national debt, there was a credibility gap in terms of how such jobs could be funded.

Also, although the Essen Council started with the case that 'the fight against unemployment and for equality of opportunity for men and women will continue to remain the paramount tasks of the European Union and its member states', its later section on Economic and Monetary Union claimed that:

> 'the first priority is to achieve the consolidation goals announced

in the national convergence programmes', then adding that: 'Above all, the structural deficits must decline in order to prevent a further increase in debt'.[12]

The outcome thereby from Essen was two contradictory priorities: job creation and deflation, with the first only to follow the second. Prioritising debt and deficit reductions without a parallel recovery through social and environmental investments to Europe, or showing that Europe could 'add value' by funding them without this counting on national debt, also had predictable results. With the epitaph delivered later, not only from the onset of the Eurozone crisis and increasing disillusion with the European project, but also in 2005 when the French and Dutch electorates rejected the Giscard Constitution for Europe less because they were 'against' the EU than because they wanted a more social Europe, and one that would 'better defend national interests'.[13]

Moreover, just before the onset of the Eurozone crisis, a group of nine member states issued an open declaration in February 2007 calling for promotion of a social Europe. France, Italy, Spain, Cyprus, Bulgaria, Luxembourg, Hungary, Belgium and Greece signed a two-page declaration in which they argued that a Europe of 27 member states 'cannot just be a free trade zone but shall guarantee the necessary balance between economic freedom and social rights'.

They also called on the European Commission, European Parliament and member states to work out a future for Social Europe by promoting reforms and adaptations related to globalisation, industrial restructuring, technological innovations, demography and migration.[14]

Yet in calling for the European Commission, European Parliament and member states to work out a future for Social Europe this displaced that the European Commission already had done so in the Delors 1993 White Paper on *Growth, Competitivenes, Cohesion.*

Commission Displacement and Denial

When the Commission, more than two years into the Eurozone crisis, finally addressed the issue of bond finance, it did so only in terms of bonds for stability rather than also for growth or sustainable development.[15]

Its report on these also brazenly claimed that the concept of a European bond 'first surfaced' in a report from one of its own committees in a 'Giovannini Group', in 2000. It then referred to publication, in September 2008, of a discussion paper issued by the European Primary Dealers Association entitled 'A Common European Government Bond' of which, like the report from the 'Giovannini Group', near to no one had ever heard.

Besides which, the Commission's case for 'A Common European Government Bond' both was a misnomer and misleading. Whereas the case of the Delors White Paper had been precisely that bonds should not be either issued or backed by governments, but European, and not counting on national debt.

For the Commission also to claim that there was no earlier discussion by Member States of bonds not only was wrong, but also displaced both Delors' own recommendation to issue common bonds – Union Bonds – in the Commission White Paper of December 1993 on *Growth, Competitiveness and Employment,* and also serial proposals by heads of state and government in more than a decade and a half to act on them.

Mitterrand, Rocard and Recovery

For example, thanks to Andreas Papandreou, recovery bonds were on the agenda of the Corfu European Council in June

1994. Luxembourg and The Netherlands were in favour. Helmut Kohl, not yet realising that Union Bonds would not be paid for by German taxpayers, was against. François Mitterrand had some reservations. With Germany against, and France at the time uncommitted, other member states did not enter the debate, and there was no vote.

But Mitterrand then changed his mind later in the year when Michel Rocard, at the time leader of the French Socialist Party, had been briefed on the case for Union Bonds. This followed my co-option as a member of the economic committee of the French Socialist Party to explain the rationale behind the Delors' 1993 proposal. On the committee, Michel Sapin, who recently had been and now is French finance minister, then volunteered:

> 'Stuart, none of this was evident at the Edinburgh European Council. When bonds were raised John Major was told that they would mean that the British taxpayer would not to have to finance the high speed rail network from Madrid to Felipe Gonzalez' constituency in Andulacia'.[16]

But the economic committee of the French Socialist Party endorsed the case for recovery bonds issued by the European Investment Fund, and Michel Rocard then called for a 50 billion ECU *European Fund for Jobs*, financed by them, at the autumn conference of the French Socialist Party, which is among the reasons why he has supported *The Modest Proposal* by Yanis Varoufakis, myself and James Galbraith, appended to this volume. When questioned by the press on whether he supported this, François Mitterrand replied:

> 'I agree with him completely, and would even go so far as to say – *and I have checked this with the Commission this morning* – that his figure could be doubled. If 100 billion ECU were made available to develop European infrastructure, we could show that Europe can be a key factor in promoting growth, work and jobs.'[17]

Mitterrand thereby gained confirmation from the Commission that a bond-financed European recovery programme was entirely feasible. When challenged on this by the President of France, the Commission could not readily deny it. But, thereafter, intimidated by an increasingly hegemonic Germany, it has not overtly denied, but entirely displaced the case for such financing of an entirely feasible European recovery programme.

Turning Helmut Kohl

While in 1995 Delors retired from the Presidency of the Commission, the case for bonds to finance a European recovery none the less survived him on the European Council. Eurobonds were on the agenda of the June 1996 Florence European Council. Jacques Chirac and Romano Prodi called for them not only to finance growth and jobs but also to underpin what at the time was the projected single currency.

Helmut Kohl initially had opposed bonds when the Portuguese Prime Minister Antonio Guterres proposed in the European Council in 1996 that the European Investment Bank should be given a cohesion and convergence remit to extend its bond finance for infrastructure projects to investments in health, education, urban renewal and finance for small and medium firms.

Kohl was opposed on the grounds that 'the German taxpayer has paid enough'. He did not understand that a bond was not a fiscal transfer but a fixed interest borrowing instrument. This also neglected that German taxpayers did not need to pay to service a European bond since other member states could do so from their own tax revenues rather than fiscal transfers to them from Germany.

But he then learned up, which was substantially due to Antonio Guterres' adviser on foreign affairs, José de Freitas Ferraz. At a meeting of the three of us in Antonio's office in Lisbon, José pointed out that he had been at the Organization for Economic Cooperation and Development (OECD) some years earlier with an adviser to Kohl and suggested we draft a minute that he might pass to the Chancellor outlining that EIB bonds did not imply fiscal transfers from Germany, and were useful for German pension funds in translating precautionary savings into interest earning project finance.

The message got through. At the following Amsterdam European Council, in spring 1997, Helmut Kohl agreed to the extension of the terms of reference of the European Investment Bank, which aided it from then until the financial crisis a decade later to quadruple its bond finance for investments, to the point at which this not only was four times the investment finance of the World Bank but also equivalent to two-thirds of the Commission's own resources without needing the fiscal transfers on which 'own resources' were based.[18]

At the 1997 Amsterdam European Council, his first, Tony Blair also initially was opposed to bonds. Yet, by the later Luxembourg Council the same year, like Helmut Kohl, he had changed his mind.[19] The Delors proposal of bond finance still was on the agenda of successive European Councils and the Ecofin finance ministers' councils thereafter. Such as when Giulio Tremonti, when finance minister of Italy from 2001, strongly and persistently recommended bonds in Ecofin on the lines proposed by Delors, although Germany still was opposed.

There also was a call by Manuel Barroso and Tony Blair, in Lisbon in February 2003, for bonds to finance a 10 year programme to create the 15 million jobs which was the employment growth target of the 1993 Delors White Paper. As well as the statement by Manuel Barroso on the re-launching, in 2005, of the Lisbon Agenda that:

'It's about growth and about jobs. This is the most urgent issue facing Europe today. We must restore dynamic growth which can bring back full employment and provide a sound base for social justice and opportunity for all'.[20]

All of this was before the 'later 1990s' to which the Commission Green Paper of 2011 on Stability Bonds wrongly attributed the 'first discussion' by Member States of 'the common issuance of bonds'. Whereas, despite Manuel Barroso having pronounced in 2003 that 'it's about growth and about jobs', by 2011 he had displaced this and lapsed into consent with an already emerging German hegemony insisting on stability rather than growth that he apparently did not feel he could contest.

Thus, neither Manuel Barroso's earlier stress on social justice nor his claim of the need for dynamic growth featured in the 2011 Commission Green Paper on 'Stability Bonds'.[21] The word 'social' appeared only once in it, in a footnote referring to the title of a document from the European Parliament. The words 'employment' and 'justice' did not appear at all. Other than in a reference to the Stability and Growth Pact, the word 'growth' appeared only once in submitting that lower interest rates could 'underpin the longer-term growth potential of the economy' which, in Keynesian terms, is as useful as pushing on a piece of string.

Notes

1. Delors achieved the right for social partners to propose policies rather than relying on the Commission to do so. This was through the so-called Val Duchesse framework, and which later was embodied in a Treaty provision allowing that: (1) that should management and labour so desire, the dialogue between them at Community level may lead to contractual relations including agreements and, (2) that this may refer to but does not depend on

a proposal from the Commission to the Council. To his discredit, Manuel Barroso as later President of the Commission neither invoked this nor even chaired any meeting on the basis of the Treaty commitments to the Val Duchesse proposals.
2. The Berlaymont headquarters of the Commission.
3. Europe 1992: *The Benefits of a Single Market. The Overall Challenge* (Cecchini Report). SEC (88) 524 final, 13 April 1988.
4. Understandably furious, the senior official concerned walked out. He clearly was sceptical whether I had any such remit from or direct access to Delors. When later in Brussels I handed him a copy of the cohesion report he declared that he would ensure that it never reached him, whereas, I was glad to be able to tell him that it already had.
5. Cecchini Report (1988). Op. cit.
6. Ibid.
7. Holland, S. (1993). *The European Challenge: Economic and Social Cohesion in the 1990s.* Foreword Jacques Delors. Nottingham: Spokesman.
8. EU Commission (1993). *Growth, Competitiveness, Employment: The Challenge and Ways Forward into the 21st Century.* COM 93 700 Final. Brussels: December 5th.
9. Delors cites in detail the approval for the White Paper by most of the then heads of state or government in his memoirs. On its being the 'high point' of his presidency, see further Hutton, Will (2003). *The World We're In.* London: Abacus.
10. The EIB also was competing with the EIF on support for small and medium firms. Whereon, advised of this, Antonio Guterres recommended to the Lisbon European Council in 2000, that the EIF should be brought within an EIB Group, and its remit to support SMEs reinforced. By 2012 the Group's SME support was approaching €11 billion and its average annual support for 2013-15 projected as over €13 billion.
11. European Council (1994). Presidency Conclusions. Essen. December.
12. European Council (1994), Ibid.
13. Manchin, (2005). *After the Referenda.* Op. cit.
14. Mahony, H. (2007). Nine states call for revival of social Europe. Brussels: eurobserver, February 15th.

70 *Beyond Austerity*

15. European Commission (2011). *Feasibility of Introducing Stability Bonds*. Green Paper. COM (2011). November 20th.
16. By the time of the Edinburgh European Council, in 1992, Delors had seen the initial statement of the case for bonds in my interim report to him on economic and social cohesion.
17. Mitterrand (1994). *L'Heure de Verité*. France 2, October 25th.
18. By 2009 total EIB lending was €82 billion. From then on to 2012, with falling co-finance from EU governments this had fallen to €44 billion. With an increase by governments in its subscribed capital in 2012 it recovered from this to €62 billion in 2013 and projected maintaining this at an annual average of €60 billion to 2015. (Joint Commission-EIB Report to the European Council, 27-28 June, 2013). But this was still dependent on and constrained by national co-finance which counted on national debt and deficits, whereas co-finance through bonds issued by the EIF, and recycling global surpluses, as part of its initial design aim, would not.
19. On being challenged by Antonio Guterres on why he initially opposed, Tony Blair replied that he had been 'briefed to do so' for any new European financial instruments. By the Luxembourg European Council later that year he had changed his mind.
20. Striedinger, A and Uhart, B. (Eds.) (2006). The EU Lisbon Agenda – An Introduction. Brussels: ESIB, p.10.
21. European Commission (2011). Feasibility of Introducing Stability Bonds. Op cit.

Chapter 4

Regress: from Delors to Juncker

A main theme of this book is the feasibility of a European New Deal jointly funded by bonds issued by the European Investment Bank and its sister institution, the European Investment Fund. But, unlike the US New Deal of the 1930s, without needing fiscal federalism or, therefore, a United States of Europe. While also stressing that, until the onset of the financial crisis, the lending for investment by the European Investment Bank already was four times that of the World Bank.

Yet, as is addressed in *The Modest Proposal* – why bonds from both the European Investment Bank and its sister institution, the European Investment Fund?

One reason is that the European Investment Bank has a 'house rule' that it only finances half of an investment project. This made sense during an earlier era of full or high employment before the eurozone crisis, when access to borrowing was not constrained by Stability Pacts and austerity. The EIB also is highly sensitive about the AAA rating of its bonds since about a third of them are purchased by pension funds, which need this to fulfil their statutory obligations to investors, whereas the rest in the main are subscribed by central banks.

The EIB also has no obligation to undertake a macroeconomic role such as the recycling of global surpluses, despite this now being vital both to co-fund European recovery and for such a recovery to offset the decline in the growth of China, which hitherto had been crucial for export-led growth for Germany, France, Italy and Spain.

Whereas such a role can be played by the European Investment Fund, as I proposed to Delors, which the European Council agreed to set up in 1994, and can gain resonance now by its co-financing EIB bonds for a European recovery without the bonds of either counting on national debt.

Whereas also, in terms of the earlier claim that the Juncker Commission is ignorant and incompetent, as well as being suborned by Wolfgang Schäuble, it presumed that the European Investment Fund could not contribute to a bond backed investment-led recovery by a misreading of its website, rather than a correct reading of its statutes. When it can do so without any treaty revision or any revision of its statutes.

The case is synthesised in Figure 3.1, where the upper line on reducing excess national debt is not in order to meet the 60% Maastricht target, which was entirely arbitrary, since whether an economy can sustain a high debt level depends on whether it can service it, as with Japan's which has been over 200% for years. Rather than that 'excess' debt can be reduced in two key regards:

1. by recovering growth with positive investment, employment, income and fiscal multipliers.
2. by shifting national borrowing for investment in health, education, urban renewal, safeguarding the environment, and support for small and medium firms to the European Investment Bank, which does not count on national debt.

There thereby are key gains from complementary EIB-EIF bond funding including mutual advantage for not only EU member states but also in the degree to which, by jointly contributing to a recovery of the European economy, they could sustain a recovery of the global economy. As also a recovery of social rather than only market values.

Figure 3.1
An Investment-Led Recovery and a European New Deal

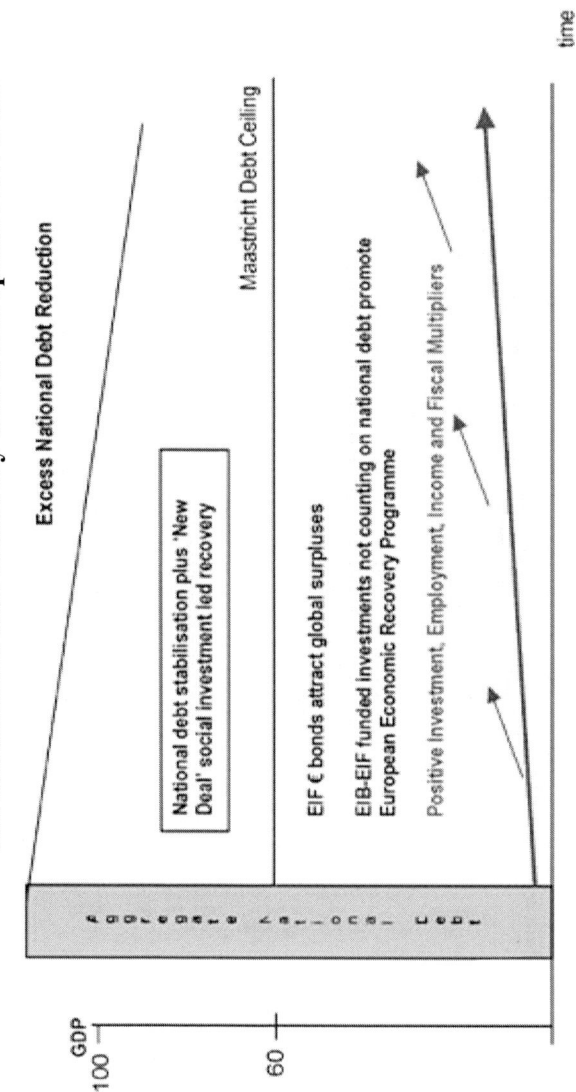

Excess National Debt Reduction

Maastricht Debt Ceiling

National debt stabilisation plus 'New Deal' social investment led recovery

EIF € bonds attract global surpluses

EIB-EIF funded investments not counting on national debt promote European Economic Recovery Programme

Positive Investment, Employment Income and Fiscal Multipliers

GDP
100
60

time

Note: A social investment led recovery programme as called for in the 2012 Economic and Social Committee Report *Restarting Growth*. EIB investment areas since 1997 include health, education, urban regeneration, environment, green technology and trans-european transport and communication networks. Multipliers generate higher investment, employment, income, and direct and indirect tax revenue.

First, in terms of social economy rather than profit maximisation, both the Bank and the Fund are non-profit public institutions which, therefore, do not need to pay dividends to their shareholders, which are the Member States of the EU.

Second, that the terms of reference of their statutes are open ended and, in the case of the European Investment Fund, to 'contribute to the pursuit of Community objectives' which, if neglected so far, can be defined by the European Council, and can include recovery of higher levels of employment and rising standards of living, which was one of the first commitments of the 1957 Rome Treaty.

Third, that, whereas the EIB is highly dependent on pension funds, EIF bonds can recycle global surpluses from global sovereign wealth funds, which may be less concerned about stock market ratings than that Europe should recover to sustain global demand.

Fourth, on the precedent that EIB borrowing is not counted on national debt, and since the EIF now is within the EIB Group, its bonds need not do so.

Fifth, that while the EIF has limited expertise of project finance, the EIB has vast experience of it, and would retain both evaluation and monitoring of projects co-financed by EIF bond issues recycling global surpluses.

Sixth, that EIF bonds can finance a European Venture Capital Fund, including new high tech start-ups, which had been one of its original design aims and welcomed in the 2012 report, *Restarting Growth,* from both trades union and employer representatives, including those of German employers.

Support from European Trades Unions and Employers

In 2009, I was invited by John Monks, at the time Secretary

General of the European Trades Union Confederation (ETUC), to meet with several of its officials to discuss alternatives to the deflation and austerity which were emerging as the main response of EU institutions to the financial crisis.

John and I had known each other when we were drafting what emerged as the economic programme of the Labour Party in 1972 and 1973. He also knew that I had been devising financial instruments and other policies for Delors.

The initial meeting led to another to which most trades unions in the EU sent representatives. They were struck by the case that recovery could be achieved without new institutions, without Treaty revisions, without national guarantees for EIB-EIF bonds, without fiscal transfers between member states and, therefore, without waiting for federalism.

This then became a statement on the case for a European New Deal for the 2010 Congress of the ETUC in Athens, which John invited me to present at its openinng plenary session.[1] Following which, a former senior member of the Italian UGT trades union, Gisolo Cedrone, persuaded the Economic and Social Committee of the European Union – social partners and representatives of civil society – to invite me to prepare a paper for them on the case.

The working group of the committee started in 2011 and, after its first meeting, invited representatives of the European Investment Bank and European Investment Fund to attend. Its chair then asked them whether it was correct that the EIF could issue bonds without a revision of its statutes. To which, conveniently, they each replied with one word – 'Yes'. Then added that, to be effective, bond issues by the European Investment Fund on a significant scale would need an increase in its subscribed capital above its current low base of only €4.5

billions but that this would need only a decision by finance ministers to do so.

The resulting report, *Restarting Growth – Two Innovative Proposals,*[2] made the case for mutualising debt up to the Maastricht 60% limit, and for recovery bonds through the EIF which could recycle global surpluses. It was overwhelmingly supported not only by the trades union representatives, but also by employers' representatives, including all of those from Germany and Philippe de Beck, president of the EU Employers' Organisation, *Business Europe,* and then was endorsed by a two-thirds majority in the next plenary session of the Committee.

The German employer representatives were especially in favour of the proposal, which had been in the initial draft for the European Investment Fund, that a share of its bonds should finance a European Venture Capital Fund for small and medium firms, and especially for new high tech start-ups.

False Start for the Juncker Recovery Agenda

One of the points forcefully made by Jean-Claude Juncker and Giulio Tremonti in a *Financial Times* article in December 2010 was that net issues of eurobonds would attract surpluses from the central banks of emerging economies and sovereign wealth funds.[3] Yet this perspective is missing from the November 2015 Commission proposal for a European Fund for Strategic Investments (EFSI), nor fulfils the commitment by Jean-Claude in his adoption address to the European Parliament in July 2015 for a €300 billion EIB bond backed investment recovery.[4]

The intention to create a European Fund for Strategic Investments echoed the case of Polish finance minister Mateusz Szczurek in an address, in September 2014, to the Bruegel Institute in

Brussels that six years had already passed since the start of the financial crisis and European GDP still was well below its pre-crisis level and around 10% below the level consistent with trend growth before the crisis. As a continent, Europe was doing worse than Japan in the aftermath of its financial meltdown of the 1980s, and worse than during the Great Depression in the 1930s. A timid recovery had recently stalled. Unemployment and the negative output gap were at record highs.[5]

Szczurek then called for an EU-wide public investment programme to overcome the constraints of Europe's 'secular stagnation'. He calculated that €700 billion of capital expenditures could close the output gap in the medium term while increasing long-term productivity growth. He also submitted that this could be funded by a special-purpose vehicle within the EIB Group, i.e. a European Fund for Strategic Investments.

Yet Szczurek wrongly claimed that this role could not be fulfilled by the European Investment Fund. As he put it:

'The EFSI's size, its direct investment in infrastructure and long-term investing horizon would be the key differences with the existing European Investment Fund, which has only 4.5 billion euros of capital and facilitates SME's access to finance through intermediary institutions with a shorter investment horizon'.

But this was a *Gestalt* misperception, in how the diminished role of the EIF had been misperceived by him or his advisors on reading its website. For Article 2.1 of the European Investment Fund's statutes determines that: 'The task of the Fund shall be to contribute to the pursuit of Community objectives', of which the stability of the Eurozone is one and a recovery of investment and employment is another.

Intentionally, in my advice to Delors, this term of reference for the European Investment Fund was as wide as the original open-ended remit for the EIB, i.e. projects of general European interest. There is no reference in the EIF's statutes to it being limited to financial support for SMEs.

Article 2.2 of the EIF's statutes specifies that: 'The activities of the Fund may include borrowing operations'. This enables it to undertake its own bond issues which were to have been the EU Bonds that Delors recommended in his December 1993 White Paper.

Both the EIB and the EIF had confirmed in evidence to the Economic and Social Committee for its 2012 Own Opinion Initiative *Restarting Growth* that the EIF could issue bonds to finance an investment-led recovery – and for a European Venture Capital Fund rather than only financial guarantees for SMEs – without a revision of its statutes or a new proposal from the Commission.[6]

Meanwhile, following a mid-September 2014 informal finance ministers meeting, European economy and industry ministers met in Brussels on September 25th to discuss practicalities. For Juncker, as he made plain in his address in July to the European Parliament before endorsement as President of the Commission, boosting the EIB's capital was crucial.

On which Werner Hoyer, the EIB's president and a former German European Affairs minister, had commented that 'expectations are somewhat exuberant' on what the bank can do to help restart the European economy and called for budgetary commitments if the EIB is to assume bigger risks in financing investments. None the less, he qualified this by stating that: 'It's clear that the EU bank (EIB) has to play a role in such a situation'.[7]

Emmanuel Macron, French industry minister, was proposing not to boost the EIB from the EU budget, as Hoyer wished, but to access and deploy unused resources from the European Stability Mechanism (ESM), the €80 billion fund set up earlier in the eurozone crisis to bail out states on the verge of bankruptcy. Rightly citing the complement of the European Investment Fund and the European Investment Bank, and investment multipliers, a French official speaking to reporters on his behalf on September 25th said that:

> 'If we could mobilise €20 to €40 billion from the ESM, for example to recapitalise the EIF, you then have a multiplier effect on the EIB that can reach almost €200 billion of public money'.[8]

But using the bailout fund was challenged by Wolfgang Schäuble, who asserted opposition to deploy ESM money to help boost growth and job creation, claiming that:

> 'The €80 billion in the European bailout scheme are not at the disposal of all possible creative ideas. They are a provision to ensure the European currency remains stable and retains the confidence of financial markets'.[9]

But the European Stability Mechanism is not written in stone. As a report for the European Parliament affirmed, it is not excluded that it undertake 'extra tasks' to ensure the stability of the Eurozone for which an investment-led recovery is vital.[10]

'Fake Money'

Meanwhile, in reaction to Wolfgang Schäuble's opposition, there also was concern in France that the €300 billion recovery plan could end up being 'fake money' in the sense of recycled funds drawing from existing programmes.[11] Which proved to be the case, even though the funds concerned, rescheduled from the Commission's 'own resources' research budget, in macroeconomic terms were miniscule. The other risk was that the fund, once created, would be hampered because of excessively strict conditions attached to its use.[12]

By November 2015, the initial EIB bond backed €300 billion recovery programme of Jean-Claude Juncker's commitment to the European Parliament only four months earlier had been reduced to €5 billion from the EIB and €16 billion from rescheduled research funds from the Commission's 'own resources' for the EFSI. This, therefore, is not primarily bond-driven, but a private finance initiative or PFI. These are notorious for seeking public guarantees and then costing more than direct public finance. A giant recovery programme had been dwarfed.

Not Needing New Criteria

The proposed European Fund for Strategic Investments aimed to invite a panel of up to eight part-time experts to determine criteria for investment projects. But there is no need to determine new criteria. Apart from the Essen European Council of 1994 defining these for Trans-European Transport and Communications Networks – which can include the ambition for a European broadband network – the Amsterdam Special Action Programme of 1997 had gained the agreement of the EIB to a cohesion and convergence remit by which it would invest in:

- Health
- Education
- Urban regeneration
- Safeguarding the environment, including green technologies
- Finance for small and medium firms

These cover a vast range of potential investment projects. Urban regeneration alone can mean renovation of buildings, new building, new public transport including trams and metro systems, electricity, gas and water supply systems, and thereby a recovery of private sector construction and engineering. Investment in health can mean renovation or extension of hospitals and health centres. In education, the same for schools, technical colleges or universities.

In a meeting arranged for me in Brussels by Jean-Paul Juncker's chef-de-cabinet, Martin Selmayr, in March 2015, it emerged the official engaged in devising new criteria for European Fund for Strategic Investment was entirely unaware of these Essen and Amsterdam Special Action Programme criteria which already had been endorsed by European Councils, excusing this on the grounds that they 'were before my time'. Which was displacement rather than denial. Yet if an institution such as the Commission, at the highest level, displaces key decisions made by earlier European Councils, it undermines not only its own legitimacy but also that of the European project.

While, also, as Mateusz Szczurek has lamented, the intended EFSI, unlike his initial proposal, has next to no bond finance. Its expected leverage or multiplier of 15, as Commissioner Jyrki Katainen since has recognised, is far too high, and has recommended it should be reduced to 5, but this, without significant public co-finance, is fantasy.

Potential Investment Multipliers

That a bond financed investment recovery did not need new institutions nonetheless was endorsed in a paper in 2014 from the Robert Schuman Foundation. The paper was exceptional also in stressing, in detail, the complementary roles of the European Investment Bank and the European Investment Fund, and including evidence that EIB investment projects could yield multipliers of 2.5 to 3. This confirmed earlier findings on investment multipliers in the UK from Blot, Creel, Rifflart and Schweisguth.[13]

A paper from the *Centre de Recherche Français dans le Domaine de l'Economie International,* in July 2013, also had been excellent in employing a neo-Keynesian model while recognising that recovery driven by public investment generates further investment and income in the private sector through multipliers, and in analytic terms went well beyond a short-term Keynesian demand management rationale.

Yet it proposed an entirely unneeded major institutional reform to create a Eurosystem of Investment Banks (ESIB), around a pan-European financial capacity that would coordinate the actions of the national public investment banks of Euro area member states. Plus a new 'Fede Fund' to be created by restructuring the European Investment Bank into 'a truly federal entity'. The Fund would orchestrate the joint work of national investment and development banks.[14]

Without Needing New Institutions

All of which, as the paper admitted, would need a Treaty revision. Which would delay recovery by negotiating such institutional changes even if there were political support for them. Yet none of which are needed since the EIB – and EIF – already have the institutional framework and statutory powers to promote recovery, while the EIB already had signed strategic partnerships with the French Public Investment Bank (BPI) and the *Caisse des Dépôts et Consignations* (CDC) and with other credit institutions in other member states.

In March 2014, an *Initiative Citoyenne Européenne* (ICE) registered a project with the Commission called NewDeal4Europe. This had been proposed by European federalists on the initiative of the Italian *Movimento Federalista Europeo* (MFE) and aimed for a European plan for sustainable development and job creation. It quickly gained support from 111 MEPs but with little reference to and therefore little learning up from the precedent of the US New Deal nor reference to the fact that EIB bonds, like US Treasury bonds, need not count on the debt of member states.[15]

Thus, the NewDeal4Europe project anticipated project bonds of up to €50 billion per year and, with a multiplier of nearly 3, giving a total investment of at least 130 billion per year for 3 years. Yet the aspiration of the project that these should be based solely on new resources of the Union displaces that these are politically implausible. Such as a financial transactions tax and a carbon tax.

Both of these are excellent proposals. But the German and Austrian initiative for a financial transactions tax so far had gained the support of 11 out of 28 member states and, while feasible, hardly has gained public resonance. A carbon tax would be likely to be opposed by Germany, granted that Wolfgang Schäuble had claimed that Germany had done enough on the environment and, since cancellation of its nuclear power programmes, had been burning brown coal to generate electricity. Its third source of finance would be a new European Value Added Tax, which might raise resources for investment but, in the interim, would further depress demand and be socially regressive.

Whereas in the US New Deal, Roosevelt did not raise taxes but shifted disposable savings into social and environmental investments. And got the programmes to initiate this deployed in its first hundred days.

In supporting the NewDeal4Europe, Bernadette Segol, who

had succeeded John Monks at the ETUC, made what in principle was an astute observation in an address to the European Parliament in claiming that:

> 'The EIB often is blocked by lack of national 'co-financing' in view of the lack of disposable resources in the most indebted member states as an outcome of seeking to respect the criteria of the Stability Pact'.[16]

But this overlooked the case already made by the ETUC in its 2010 Athens Congress statement, and in the 2012 report *Restarting Growth* from trades unions and employers representatives on the Economic and Social Committee, that EIB co-financing need not be national since its sister institution in the EIB Group – the EIF – can provide this by issuing its own bonds and that its lending for investment, as with EIB bonds, need not count on national debt.

Recycling Global Surpluses

There is no global dimension to the Juncker proposal for the misnamed European Fund for Strategic Investments, which near to entirely lacks any funding. This is despite recovery of the European economy being vital for the rest of the world economy. Whereas this is entirely feasible through European Investment Fund bonds recycling global surpluses from pension funds and sovereign wealth funds.

Such recycling not only was advocated in 2010 by Jean-Claude Juncker and Giulio Tremonti in their making the case for eurobonds. The South African minister of finance, Nhlanhla Nene, declared at the meeting of the BRICS in Washington on 25 September 2014, that they would invest in eurobonds if these were to finance a European recovery.[17]

Moreover, while governments in the EU have feared both rating agencies and bond markets, when Standard & Poor downgraded Eurozone member states' debt in January 2012, it stressed that key reasons were simultaneous debt and spending reductions by governments and households, the weakening thereby of economic growth, and inability of European policymakers to assure an economic recovery.[18]

A Bain and Company Global Private Equity Report for 2012 stressed that, from the summer of 2011, a cavalcade of bad news in Western Europe and the United States had thrown private equity activity into reverse. Almost $2 trillion of equity funds were seeking but not finding such outlets, while pension funds, endowments, foundations and many other private partners need such investment outlets and returns to meet liquidity demands on their portfolios. In its 2013 report, Bain stressed that private equity investments faced an intensely competitive deal-making environment worldwide, with an overhang of assets needing to be invested. Its 2014 report headlined that low growth still was blocking such investments.[19]

In 2013, Bill Gross, at the time head of the trillion dollar Pimco pension fund, also called for European recovery, stressing that pension funds needed growth to secure retirement incomes, whereas low to near-zero interest rates in Europe would not. Sovereign wealth funds also have been affected by the failure of Europe to offset national debt and deficit reduction by bond finance for recovery. In March 2012, the Norwegian minister of finance announced that Norway's sovereign wealth fund, the world's biggest and hitherto Europe's major private sector investor, would reduce its European commitments from over half to two-fifths while raising investments in emerging markets and Asia-Pacific from just over a tenth to two-fifths.[20]

Asian sovereign wealth funds have over $3 trillion in assets that also need investment outlets, and are seeking them internationally. The China Investment Corporation (CIC) is the largest single fund, at some half a trillion dollars. Yet the CIC was far from immune from the weakness of growth in Europe and the US. In 2011, it made a loss on its private equity investments, cut its holdings of private securities to a quarter, and announced that it was seeking longer-term public sector investments, with a return period of 10 years or more.[21]

What is striking about the CIC's announcement is that it coincides precisely with the case for Europe to attract such surpluses by issuing bonds to finance the long term public investments for which the European Investment Bank has had a remit since the 1997 Amsterdam Special Action Programme, i.e. in health, education, urban renewal, safeguarding the environment, and support for small and medium firms, which enabled it to quadruple its investments from then until the onset of the Eurozone crisis.

In September 2015, China announced that it would invest from €5 to €10 billion in EFSI projects.[22] But €5 to €10 billion is not a macroeconomic figure. By the same date some member states had declared that they also would invest. But all of the projects they proposed were in infrastructure, not in the social cohesion areas that had been the basis of the extension of the terms of reference of the EIB in the Amsterdam Special Action programme of 1997, i.e. health, education, urban regeneration and the environment.[23]

As Jérôme Vignon, a former deputy director of the Commission's Forward Studies Unit, has submitted, the 'rich legacy' of the Delors 1993 White Paper on *Growth, Competitiveness, Employment*, which Delors regarded as the high point of his Presidency of the Commission thereby, so far, has gone by default.[24] In particular, as Vignon has stressed, through neglect of the proposal in the White Paper of Union bonds and European Investment Fund recovery bonds. Recognition of the feasibility of a New Deal for Europe, which was integral to the proposal for joint EIB-EIF bonds is also still entirely feasible within existing institutions, without Treaty revisions, without national guarantees, without new investment criteria, and without fiscal transfers between member states.

Notes

1. ETUC Congress (2010). The ETUC Will Fight For A European New Deal. May 19th. https://www.etuc.org/…/etuc-congress-approves-athens…
2. Economic and Social Committee. (2012). Restarting Growth: Two Innovative Proposals. ces474-2012_ac_en and also in other European languages.
3. Juncker, J-C and Tremonti, G. (2010). €-bonds would end the crisis. *The Financial Times*, December 5th.
4. Jean-Claude Juncker (2014). A New Agenda for Jobs, Growth, Fairness and Democratic Change. Statement to the European Parliament, July 15th.
5. Szczurek, M. (2014). Investing for Europe's Future. Address to the Bruegel Institute. Brussels: September 4th.
6. Economic and Social Committee (2012), Op. cit.
7. Buergin, R. (2014). Hoyer Warns of Exuberant Expectations of EIB's Role in Recovery. Bloomberg Business Week, September 13th.
8. Les Echos. (2014) Plan d'investissements: Paris veut utiliser le fonds de secours européen. September 25th. Euroactiv (2014).
9. Reuters (2014). 'Berlin slams Commerzbank CEO for urging eurozone bonds'. September 3rd.
10. De Witte, B. (2012). European Stability Mechanism and Treaty on Stability, Coordination and Governance: Role of the EU Institutions and Consistency with the EU Legal Order, European Parliament.
11. Euroactiv (2014). 'French wary of "fake money" in EU's €300bn investment plan'. September 26th

12. Emmanuel Macron. Cit. Euroactiv, ibid.
13. Fondation Robert Schuman (2014). Pour une relance de l'investissement en Europe. September 22nd. Blot, C, Creel, J, Rifflart, C. and Schweisguth, D. (2009) Petit manuel de stratégie de sortie de crise: Paris: Observatoire Français des Conjonctures Economiques.
14. Valla, N. Brand, T. and Doisy, S. (2014). New Architecture for Public Investment in Europe. CEPII Policy Brief N° 4, July.
15. Fabre, F. Cazanave, F. and Billion, J-F. (2014). Les *limit*es* du Plan Juncker d'investissements de l'Union européenne et les supériorités de l'ICE « NewDeal4europe » en matière de ressources propres de l'Union européenne. Le Taurillon, September 15th.
16. Segol (July 25th. 2014) http://euractiv.fr/sections/priorites-ue-2020/les-eurodeputes 37.
17. Holland, S. (2015). The Delors Agenda, the Juncker Agenda and a European New Deal. Paper to the European Economic and Social Committee of the EU, June.
   http://www.eesc.europa.eu/?i=portal.en.industry-monetary-policy-documents.36006
18. The Telegraph. (2012), 'Standard & Poor's cuts ratings of nine Eurozone countries'. Op. cit.
19. Bain & Company. Global Private Equity Reports, 2012, 2013, 2014.
20. 'Norway's $610 bn wealth fund to cut Europe exposure'. March 30th.
   Private Equity Intelligence (2013) *Sovereign Wealth Fund Review*. October. https://www.preqin.com/…/2013-preqin www.pionline.com/…/a-year-later-pimco-still-feels-e…
21. http://www.upi.com/Business_News/2012/07/25/Chinas-sovereign-wealth-fund-reports-loss/
22. Valero, J. (2015). 'China uses Juncker Plan to boost involvement in Europe'. EuroActiv.com October 6th.
23. Valero. ibid.
24. Vignon, J. (2014). 'The Rich Legacy of the White Paper on Growth, Competitiveness and Employment'. Tribune, February 13th.

Chapter 5
Beyond a German Europe

Jean Monnet is renowned for claiming that 'Europe will be forged in crises, and will be the sum of the solutions adopted for those crises'. Yet his supranational design *caused* serial crises in the postwar European project.

Such as the supranationalism that led Attlee to reject the Monnet proposal for a Coal and Steel Community and that divided Europe thereafter from 1957 into a European Community and a European Free Trade Area for nearly two decades. Also a deepening democratic deficit such as, well before the Eurozone crisis, the recycling as a Lisbon Treaty of a Constitution which had been rejected by the only electorates to whom it had been put.

With also a persistent social deficit by displacing the commitment to rising standards of living of the 1957 Rome Treaty, and to economic and social cohesion in its first revision in the 1986 Single European Act.

Writing in 2015 in relation to Monnet's claim that crises are the occasion for further integration, Philippe Legrain has commented on the conventional wisdom in Brussels that deeper integration is needed with a fiscal and political union, to complete the monetary one. But also has asked, in a manner paralleling *Europe in Question and what to do about it,* what if deeper integration, if achievable at all, would actually be a mistake?[1]

A mistake not only in terms of economic effectiveness, but in terms of the shift from erosion to outright denial of national democracy. As has been the case with the Eurogroup of eurozone finance ministers blatantly denying the outstanding 'No' to austerity in the July referendum in Greece and in the next few hours deepening its austerity demands.

A mistake also in terms of public opinion. Thus an August 2015 survey by Opinium Research found that whereas near half of those polled in Italy and over half in Spain and Portugal favoured 'ever closer union', only 24% of those polled in France, and only 17% of those polled in the Netherlands did so. A quarter of those in Italy, over 30% in France, and over 40% of those in the UK and the Netherlands wanted to repatriate powers to national governments. While opinion in the UK whether to stay or leave the EU is finely balanced.[2]

This chapter also indicates that there have been increasing divisions within the Troika of the IMF, the ECB and the Commission, with the IMF admitting that the Commission's mantra in demanding 'structural reforms' has no basis in any evidence within the OECD countries; that the Commission has under-estimated the compound negative effects of cuts in terms of beggar-my-neighbour deflation, and that its Friedmanite presumption of public spending 'crowding out' the private sector is unfounded.

But it starts by evidencing concerns from leading German politicians such as the former Chancellor Helmut Schmidt, former finance minister Oskar Lafontaine and former foreign minister Joschka Fischer that – despite denial by Wolfgang Schäuble – the 'German Question' is back and that, if not gaining an adequate response, threatens Europe as a democratic project. With an echo also by French industry minister Emmanuel Macron of the analysis in chapter 1 of the negative role of a presumptive Protestant Ethic in blocking feasible recovery.

Return of 'The German Question'

There was a tendency after WW1, yet more clearly so after WW2, to claim that it was German nationalism that had caused both. But while right in part, this was not the whole. The Franco-Prussian war of 1870-71, and the occupation thereafter of Alsace Lorraine, had political, military and economic motives which were those of élites rather than of the whole of German society.

The politics reflected the concern of Germany that it never again should be decimated by foreign powers, as it had been in the Thirty Years War. This case was well made by former German Chancellor Helmut Schmidt in one of his last public statements, a speech in 2011 that he gave to a convention of the German Social Democrats. As he put it:

> 'Whenever the states or peoples in the midst of Europe were weak its neighbours entered from the periphery to the weak centre. The biggest devastation and the greatest loss of life occurred during the 30 Years War, 1618-1648, which mostly took part on German soil.'

While Schmidt, inversely, also referred to risks when the Centre of Europe was strong. Such as that:

> 'When the dynasties or the states in the centre of Europe were strong – or when they felt strong – they then conquered the periphery. That already happened under the crusades which were also conquests. Not only in Asia Minor and Jerusalem but also in the direction of Eastern Prussia and all three Baltic states.'[3]

The outcome of this was what Schmidt appropriately deemed the 'Second Thirty Years War' from 1914 to 1945 and, in both cases, disasters.

Paralleling this analogy, in September 2015 French Industry Minister Emmanuel Macron, whose proposal for a bond-funded European recovery had been opposed by Wolfgang Schäuble, called the struggle in the Eurozone a new Thirty Years War in Europe between Calvinists and Catholics, saying that:

> 'The Calvinists want to make others pay until the end of their life. They want reforms or no contributions toward any solidarity. On the other side are the Catholics, largely on the periphery … At every eurozone summit, at every Eurogroup, we have this same dilemma between member states. We have to end this religious war.'[4]

While former German finance minister, and former president of Saarland, Oskar Lafontaine, writing in 2015, admitted that, as a convinced European, he had long supported the politics of a growing transfer of tasks towards the European level but that he now questioned this, recognising that:

> 'Thomas Mann dreamed of a European Germany. His wish has turned into its opposite. Today we have a German Europe. Democracy and decentralisation are mutually conditioning. The larger a unity, the more opaque it is, the more removed it is, the less controllable it is… One should not transfer to a higher level those things that [member states] can better manage themselves.'[5]

Former German foreign minister Joschka Fischer had echoed this only days after the rejection by Wolfgang Schäuble of the 'No vote' in the Greek referendum in July 2015. As he put it:

> 'The path that Germany will pursue in the twenty-first century – toward a 'European Germany' or a 'German Europe' – has been the fundamental historical question at the heart of German foreign policy for two centuries. And it was answered during the long night of negotiations over Greece on July 12th-13th with a German Europe prevailing over a European Germany.'

Adding that this was a fateful decision for both Germany and Europe and wondering whether Angela Merkel and Wolfgang Schäuble 'knew what they were doing'.[6]

Schäuble, Syriza and the Denial of Dialogue

At a conference in Austin Texas in November 2013, Alexis Tsipras made *The Modest Proposal* of Yanis Varoufakis, myself and James Galbraith the basis of the negotiating position of what shortly could be a Syriza government in Greece.

The essentials of *The Modest Proposal* were those that are argued throughout this volume, i.e. that a recovery of the European economy is feasible without new institutions, without Treaty changes, without fiscal transfers between member states and therefore also without federalism. And that Greece could not recover without a recovery of the rest of Europe. Plus in particular, that there should be a moratorium on repayment of Greek debt.[7]

Yet, within an hour of the victory of Syriza in the general election in January, Wolfgang Schäuble declared: 'The election alters nothing... There is no alternative to structural reforms', adding that Greece must 'stick to the rules'.

Jeroen Dijsselbloem, the Dutch president of the Eurogroup of Eurozone finance ministers, then ruled 'out of order' Syriza's case that Greek recovery depended on European recovery, and refused to allow it to be considered for discussion. Despite such a recovery being vital not only for Greece but also for the other Eurozone member states that were suffering high levels of unemployment, and especially youth unemployment and the need to reduce this rather than only reduce debt. As Varoufakis has put it:

> 'In my first week as minister for finance I was visited by Jeroen Dijsselbloem, president of the Eurogroup (the eurozone finance ministers), who put a stark choice to me: accept the bailout's "logic" and drop any demands for debt restructuring or your loan agreement will "crash" – the unsaid repercussion being that Greece's banks would be boarded up.'[8]

Yet, while Wolfgang Schäuble declared that Greece must 'stick to the rules', on what authority, and by whose rules does the Eurogroup propose or decide anything? As Varoufakis has recorded:

> 'The Eurozone is run by a body (the Eurogroup) that lacks written rules of procedure, debates crucial matters "confidentially" and without minutes being taken, and is not obliged to answer to any elected body, not even the European Parliament.'[9]

Psychology was relevant in other regards in that the finance ministers of several of the member states that had already accepted austerity programmes to the cost of their own popularity were unwilling to admit that there could be alternatives.

But also in terms of inter-personal dynamics in the Eurogroup. Most of its members were not economists. When Varoufakis nonetheless made the case, some complained that he should stop lecturing them, and leaked this to the press on a coordinated basis, thereby implying that he was merely a theoretical economist whereas they were experienced politicians. Though Varoufakis knew more about feasible alternatives to austerity – as in the *Modest Proposal* – than any of them other than, perhaps, Michel Sapin, who had been briefed earlier by me on the case for a bond-backed European recovery programme when Michel Rocard had co-opted me onto the economic committee of the French Socialist Party – even if that had been years earlier.

Sapin initially supported Varoufakis on the case for relaxing the terms demanded by the Troika, yet this did not lead to dialogue but to a 'shouting match' between Sapin and Wolfgang Schäuble, with Schäuble claiming that France herself needed a Troika programme and Sapin vehemently asserting that Germany could not dictate to France.[10]

Forced Exits?

Schäuble then proposed that unless Greece complied with Berlin's demand it should leave the Eurozone. He echoed this again at an emergency Eurozone summit weekend in Brussels early in July 2015.

His move provoked another 'shouting match', with ECB president Mario Draghi. It was Draghi's pledge to do 'whatever it takes' to hold the euro together, which earlier had quelled the panic that threatened to destroy the single currency in the summer of 2012.[11] This provoked reporting that Schäuble had been opposed by Angela Merkel and that the federal government was divided on the issue.[12]

Schäuble, unilaterally, was risking this. With no counterpart provisions such as financial support from Germany or other Eurozone member states for a transitional period in which Greece, or any other member state leaving the euro, either by choice or by compulsion, could introduce an alternative currency.

Yet, thereafter, the German Council of Economic Experts, which advises the federal government, and with only the dissenting voice of Peter Bofinger, its trades union representative, proposed generalising Wolfgang Schäuble's claim that any country that breaches the fiscal rules and 'continually fails to cooperate' should exit the Eurozone. In citing this, Philippe Legrain commented that 'the message to those tempted to defy the German line could scarcely be clearer'.[13]

Before the end of Yanis Varoufakis' term as Greek finance minister, other members of the Eurogroup made plain that they would not 'negotiate' further with him and demanded his replacement, with which Alexis Tsipras concurred. While, as Yanis has stressed since his 'expulsion' from the Eurogroup –

for which there is no Treaty provision or other precedent in any European Council – the Schäuble message to Greece was designed to be a warning to other member states not only in Southern Europe, such as Spain and Portugal, but also to France, that they should not challenge the new German ideology of austerity.[14]

Yet, in relation to Joschka Fischer's question whether Angela Merkel and Wolfgang Schäuble knew what they were doing, it became evident that Schäuble had a very clear idea – a new design. This was for a limited 'inner' political union to support the euro with a formalised Eurogroup of the Eurozone's finance ministers, presided over by a president who wields veto power over national budgets and which would nominally be legitimised by a Euro Chamber of parliamentarians from the eurozone member states. In exchange for forfeiting control over their budgets, Schäuble offered the promise of a small Eurozone-wide common budget that would partly fund unemployment and deposit-insurance schemes.[15]

Whereas this did not appeal to either France or Italy. It also fulfilled the fear of former German Chancellor Helmut Schmidt in his earlier cited 2011 speech that:

> 'If we Germans let ourselves be seduced, based upon our economic strength, to demand a role of political leadership in Europe, or at least play the *primus inter pares,* a growing majority of our neighbours would effectively defend themselves against that. The worry of the periphery about a strong centre of Europe would return quite fast. The probable consequences of such a development would be crippling for the EU. And Germany would fall into isolation.'[16]

Marginalising the IMF

Under the direction of Olivier Blanchard, the Research

Department of the IMF has been remarkably open in critiquing economic theories which it earlier had espoused as a member of the Troika with the ECB and the European Commission. This included:

1. That it had under-estimated negative multipliers in the EU by a factor of up to 1.7 rather than its earlier assessment of 0.5, i.e. by less than a third of the actual deflationary effect.[17]

2. Unlike the 'crowding out' hypothesis of Milton Friedman, recent research by the IMF had found there is no evidence that public spending drains rather than sustains the private sector.[18]

3. In analysing OECD data for 27 countries, it found no negative effects on economic efficiency that result from defence of employee rights through protective labour market legislation. In other words there was *no evidence* for the case of 'structural reforms'.[19]

4. In November 2015, an IMF Staff Discussion Note published findings that 'beggar-thy-neighbour' wages policy through 'structural reforms' was not a condition for recovery but was persistently deflationary.[20] It based this on an evaluation of five countries representing 30% of the economic weight of the euro area (Italy, Spain, Portugal, Ireland and Greece).[21]

Moreover, two days after the January 25 2015 election that brought Syriza into office in Greece, *The Financial Times* published an article by Reza Moghadam, the former head of the IMF's European Department, who played a major role in the Greek crisis from 2010 to 2014, arguing that there should be a 50% reduction in Greece's debt.[22] As Paul Blustein has commented, Moghadam's article offered stark evidence of divisions that already were splitting the Troika.[23]

But, before the formation of the Troika, 'powerful Europeans' strongly resisted IMF participation in the rescue of a euro area country. IMF Managing Director Dominique Strauss-Kahn therefore had undertaken that the Fund would be a 'junior partner' in the Troika, putting up a minority share of the loans Greece needed and without strategic influence over policy.[24] Which, in turn, evidenced the reality of a German hegemony not only over other member states but also what was supposed to be the most powerful multilateral finance institution in the world.

Inhibiting the ECB

In December 2012, some of us from the Economic and Social Committee met with vice presidents and division heads of the ECB and the German member of its Executive Committee, Jörg Asmussen, to discuss the Committee's report *Restarting Growth: Two Innovative Proposals,* i.e. joint EIB-EIF bond financing of a social investment-led recovery. Asmussen openly agreed that this was vital, but claimed that it was ruled out for the ECB by its statutes and that governments needed to take the lead on it.

What then emerged was remarkable in his advocating that we, rather than the ECB, should take the initiative on this by making the case both to governments and EU central banks, which I nonetheless did by approaching the governor of the Central Bank of Portugal, Carlos da Silva Costa, and the Italian government, recommending that they circulate the case, and which Carlos da Silva Costa confirmed that he had.

Yet which implicitly indicated the degree to which German hegemony was inhibiting the ECB's own autonomy, as in Jens Weidman of the Bundesbank taking the ECB to the Karlsruhe constitutional court with claims that it already had exceeded its mandate, and on which Jörg Asmussen had been the ECB's defendent.[25]

The outcome was no synergy between the ECB and governments on the case for an investment-led recovery. Thereafter, the austerity case was reinforced when Jörg Asmussen chose to resign from the ECB to become deputy minister for industry in the CDU-CSU-SPD government, formed in 2013 after federal elections in Germany, and was replaced as German executive director of the ECB by Sabine Lautenschläger.

By November 2014, Lautenschläger had signalled opposition to the ECB purchasing government bonds of Eurozone countries unless there was a clear threat of persistent fall in consumer prices. Siding with Bundesbank President Jens Weidman, she then led opposition in the Governing Council of the ECB to the decision on 22 January 2015 of quantitative-easing through large-scale bond buying, expressing concerns that this would remove pressure from euro-area countries to reform their economies and boost competitiveness.[26]

In other words, for Lautenschläger, 'structural reforms' still ruled despite the years in which it was apparent that they had deepened deflation, which was shortly to be confirmed by the analysis four months later by the IMF that there was no evidence from 27 OECD countries that protective labour legislation inhibited economic efficiency.

In January 2015 the ECB announced an expanded Outright Monetary Transactions Programme. This included purchases of bonds issued by euro-area central governments, agencies and European institutions with the purchases intended to continue until at least September 2016, with the package designed to fulfil its price stability mandate.[27]

In April 2015, Lautenschläger publicly called into question the effectiveness of the OMT programme, including the claim that 'with low interest rates, there is a greater danger of investment behaviour becoming too risky' and that 'overheating or price bubbles can easily emerge in other asset classes'.[28] Yet which had some force. Whereas what was needed for a bond-backed recovery of investment that Jörg Asmussen had recognised when meeting with myself and others from the Economic and Social Committee in December 2012, yet which Wolfgang Schäuble had rejected and was to continue to refuse.

Compounding Commission Incompetence

The IMF had been minoritised. The ECB had been challenged by Germany and was divided. While the Commission since the onset of the Eurozone crisis has been both politically incapable and technically incompetent.

That it proved incapable was illustrated when its economic and finance commissioner, the former French finance minister Pierre Moscovici, spoke briefly with Varoufakis after an especially abrasive exchange in the Eurogroup and said: 'Yanis, if it were up to us we could solve this in minutes on the back of an envelope. But I can't'. The reasons were the degree to which Brussels had been suborned by Berlin. As Varoufakis put it to me afterwards: 'The Commission no longer counts'.

The earlier background to this was evidenced in 2014 by Philippe Legrain, after he resigned as deputy head of the Forward Planning Unit *(Cellule des Prospectives)* of Manuel Barroso, in a book entitled *European Spring: Why Our Economies and Politics are in a Mess – and How to Put Them Right*. During the latter part of the Barroso presidency of the Commission, the 'Community Method' by which the Commission should make proposals to a full Council of Ministers had been sidelined. Anything of any significance was first cleared for approval with Berlin. Nothing other than Berlin's view was on the agenda.[29]

Jean-Claude Juncker then ranked restoration of The Community Method – i.e. joint inter-governmental decision-making – high among his ten priority commitments for his endorsement as President of the Commission by the European Parliament in July 2014, of which the first was a €300 billion EIB bond-backed investment recovery programme. Yet by November this had been reduced to a private finance initiative in a European Fund for Strategic Investment, despite no other major member state than Germany being opposed to a major bond-funded investment recovery, and both France, through Emmanuel Macron, and Poland, through Mateusz Szczurek, strongly in favour
.

In doing so the Commission had entirely displaced that a European Fund for Strategic Investment was not needed since the already established European Investment Fund could do this without a new institution. It incompetently failed to recognise that, jointly, the European Investment Bank and the European Investment Fund can issue bonds that can channel global pension fund and sovereign wealth fund surpluses into investment programmes for which wide ranging criteria already have been agreed by governments.

In the interim more than a year was lost in even starting a European recovery programme. While in addition, in December 2014 at a meeting in Brussels, neither the economic adviser to European Council President Donald Tusk, nor to Commission President Jean-Claude Juncker, nor to the Employment Commissioner Marianne Thyssen, nor to the Commissioner for Jobs, Growth, Investment and Competitiveness Jyrki Katainen, nor the senior economist to the Commission were aware that EIB borrowing does not count on national debt.[30]

Troika in Question

In 2014, a report from a special inquiry into the Troika by the European Parliament submitted that 'there was no appropriate legal basis for setting up the Troika in terms of European primary law' and that its programme conditions did not respect the Charter of Fundamental Rights of the European Union.[31]

In January 2015, in an interim ruling on the legality of the European Central Bank's 2012 bond-buying plan, the European Court of Justice gave a green light for the ECB to purchase government bonds. But ruled that 'it must refrain from any direct involvement in the financial assistance programme that applies to the state concerned'. This rightly challenged the deflationary 'structural adjustment' programmes of the Troika.[32]

Economy and finance commissioner Pierre Moscovici, speaking at a Brussels-based think tank in January 2015, echoed this case, saying that the 'troika should be replaced with a more democratically legitimate and more accountable structure based around European institutions with enhanced parliamentary control'.[33]

But German finance minister Wolfgang Schäuble reacted by asserting that that he foresaw no quick end to the Troika format. He suggested that if Jean-Claude Juncker thinks differently, he should seek changes to the EU treaties, adding that: 'The German government has been tirelessly asking for such changes'.[34] Yet by what changes, and with what institutional reforms? If agreed, would they mean an end to the German hegemony that Adenauer, Brandt, Schmidt and Kohl did not want, or reinforce it?

Neither 'Southern Sinners' nor 'Northern Saints'

It has been suggested in and since chapter 1 that what underlies opposition to Eurobond finance has been the dual meaning of

Schuld as both debt and guilt, the astute observation of Nietzsche that strong German creditors not only want repayment from weak debtors but to punish them for their debt-guilt, and the deadening legacy of Weber in claiming that it was a Protestant Ethic that had caused the rise of capitalism.

This has been aptly paralleled in a paper published in 2015 by Matthias Matthijs and Kathleen McNamara in terms of northern 'saints' and southern 'sinners'. In this they address why austerity and structural reforms, as alleged cures for member states' alleged 'fiscal profligacy' and 'lack of competitiveness', won out over what they deemed by far the most potentially efficacious alternative solution to the euro's woes – the introduction and joint issuance of a common debt instrument or 'Eurobond'.[35]

Matthijs and McNamara submit that there has been only one significant 'sinner', Greece, stressing that Ireland or Spain had debt levels lower than those of Germany before the onset of the 2007-08 crisis. Yet the 'sinners' in Greece were not its working people, but German and French banks that lent without realistic prospects of repayment for purchases by Greek oligarchs and the military. As well as banks such as Goldman Sachs which, in 2001, enabled deals, some of which were similar to a second mortgage, yet which did not count on national debt.[36]

Matthijs and McNamara rightly claim – in line with *Gestalt* cases of perception or misperception – that the dominant view of the crisis was shaped by German academics, think-tanks, private and public sector actors, and powerful business and financial interests including those controlling not only the 'popular' but also 'quality' German media.

However their further claim, that such ideas 'had long

underwritten the euro's institutional design at Maastricht and Amsterdam during the euro's formative decade', displaces that the Amsterdam European Council in June 1997 also called for the European Investment Bank to invest in health, education, urban regeneration, green technology and defence of the environment, as well as financial support for small and medium firms. Which the EIB accepted and then was endorsed at the later December 1997 Luxembourg European Council. And which enabled the EIB to quadruple its lending in the next decade to four times that of the World Bank.

Moreover, regrettably reinforcing the misperception of Merkel and Schäuble, Matthijs and McNamara only consider Eurobonds in terms of mutualisation of debt, not bonds for recovery. There is no reference in their analysis either to recovery bonds or the role that can be played in issuing them by the European Investment Fund. Nor to the Delors White Paper on *Growth, Competitiveness, Employment* of 1993 and its case that the debt and deficit conditions of Maastricht could be offset by the EIF complementing EIB bonds – which by its house rule can only co-finance 50% of an investment project – by recycling global surpluses.

Nor Over Merkel's 'Dead Body'

Angela Merkel in 2012 had denied Eurobonds in principle, pronouncing that 'I don't see total [European] debt liability as long as I live' and that the idea of Eurobonds was 'economically wrong and counterproductive'.[37] Yet this 'over my dead body' opposition to Eurobonds was flawed on multiple grounds.

1. It displaced the key distinction between bonds for mutualisation of debt from bonds for recovery.

2. It neglected that the case for mutualisation of debt either by

Varoufakis and myself, in two versions of *The Modest Proposal* in 2010 and 2011, or in the Brueghel 'Blue Bond' proposal, was not for the 'total debt liability' that she assumed.[38]

3. It overlooked that, rather than 'economically wrong and counterproductive', bond finance by the German *Kreditanstalt für Wiederaufbau* – KfW – was vital in both the postwar reconstruction of Germany during the period of Marshall Aid and in funding infrastructure and other projects in the reunification of Germany.

4. It reflected no awareness that whereas KfW bonds count on the national debt of Germany, EIB bonds do not. Even if she might be excused as much since, as late as December 2014, not a single adviser to Donald Tusk, Jean-Claude Juncker or to Jyrki Katainen knew it either.

5. It implied that she was presuming that Eurobonds would need to be guaranteed, and serviced, by German taxpayers, as had been the case with Helmut Kohl initially opposing extension of the terms of reference of the EIB to fund social and environmental investments which, in both cases, was misinformed.

Thus, displacing that bonds for a European recovery need not be 'over her dead body' since Germany neither need guarantee nor service them.

Notes

1. Legrain, P. (2015). 'You Never Want a Serious Crisis to go to Waste'. The Brussels Times. September 15th. Op. cit.
2. Opinium Research (2015). ourinsight.opinium.co.uk/…opinium…/op5154_ August 15th.
3. Schmidt, H. (2011). Germany in and with Europe. library.fes.de/pdf-files/id/ipa/08888.

4. Schmidt, H. (2011). Ibid.
5. Evans-Pritchard (2015). 'Mr Macron compares the euro's plight to a new Thirty Years religious war on the continent.' The Telegraph. September 24th.
6. Lafontaine, O. (2015). Let's develop a Plan B for Europe. http://links.org.au/node/4573 September 23rd.
7. Fischer, J. (2015). The Return of the Ugly German. Project Syndicate. July 23rd.
8. Varoufakis, Y, Holland S. and Galbraith, J. K. (2014). The Modest Proposal, 4.0
9. Varoufakis, Y. (2015). 'Germany won't spare Greek pain – it has an interest in breaking us.' The Guardian July 10th
10. Varoufakis, Y. (2015). 'Democratizing the Eurozone' *Project Syndicate*. September 1st 2015
11. Legrain, P. (2015). 'You Never Want a Serious Crisis to go to Waste.' Op cit.
12. Spiegel International (2015). 'A Government Divided: Schäuble's Push for Grexit Puts Merkel on Defensive.' July 17th
13. Legrain (2015). Op cit.
14. Varoufakis, Y. (2015). 'Germany won't spare Greek pain.' Op cit.
15. Varoufakis, Y. (2015). 'Schäuble's Gathering Storm.' Social Europe. October 26th
16. Schmidt, H. (2011). Germany in and with Europe. Op. Cit.
17. Blanchard, O. and Leigh, D. (2013). IMF Working Paper WP/13/1.
18. Abiad, A. Furceri, D. and Topalova, P. (2015). The Macroeconomic Effects of Public Investment: Evidence from Advanced Economies. IMF Working Paper WP/15/95
19. Blanchard, O. and Leigh, D. (2013). Growth Forecast Errors and Fiscal Multipliers. IMF Working Paper/13/1. Auerbach, A. and Gorodnichenko, Y. (2011). Fiscal Multipliers in Recession and Expansion. National Bureau of Economic Research Working Paper 17447. Cambridge, MA.
20. IMF (2015). Wage Moderation in Crises: Policy Considerations and Applications to the Euro Area. Staff Discussion Note SDN/15/22.
21. Janssen, R. (2015). Lost In Contradiction: The IMF and Competitive Wage Dumping In The Euro Area. Social Europe.

November 27th.
22. Moghadam, R. (2015). Halve Greek debt and keep the eurozone together. The Financial Times. January 26th
23. Blustein, P. (2015). 'The Greek Crisis: Human Errors-and Divine Forgiveness?' Centre for International Governance Innovation, February 20th.
24. Blustein. Ibid.
25. Evans-Pritchard, A. (2013). 'Germany's brother gladiators battle over euro destiny in constitutional court.' Op. cit.
26. Parkin, B. and Riecher, S. (2015). 'ECB's Draghi seeks real economic union to lead euro-area reforms.' Bloomberg Business, January 24th.
27. European Central Bank. (2015). ECB announces expanded asset purchase programme. Frankfurt, January 22nd
28. 'ECB's Lautenschläger casts doubts on QE's effectiveness.' Reutershttp://www.reuters.com/article/2015/04/02/ecb-lautenschlaeger-idUSF9N0WF01I20150402#QUvXf5z5Jl8Gqwi0.99
29. Philippe Legrain (2014). *European Spring: Why Our Economies and Politics are in a Mess – and How to Put Them Right*. London: Creative Books.
30. Holland, S. (2015). 'False Start for the Juncker Recovery Proposals.' *Notas Economicas. Revista da Faculdade de Economia*, Universidade de Coimbra. June http://www.uc.pt/feuc/notas-economicas/artigos/resumos/numero_41.
31. European Parliament (2014). Report on the enquiry on the role and operations of the Troika (ECB, Commission and IMF) with regard to the euro area programme countries. 013/2277(INI)) PE 526.111v02-00 A7-0149/2014
32. Spiegel, P. and Jones, C. (2015). 'Troika in question after EU court ruling on bond-buying plan. The Financial Times. January 14th.
33. Wishart, I. (2015). 'Troika Should Be Replaced With EU Option, Moscovici Says.' Bloomberg. January 19th.
34. Popp, V. (2015). 'End-of-troika debate amplifies ahead of Greek elections.' https://euobserver.com/political/127300
35. Matthijs, M. and McNamara, K. (2015). 'The Euro Crisis' Theory Effect: Northern Saints, Southern Sinners, and the

Demise of the Eurobond.' *Journal of Economic Integration.* 37:2, 229-245, DOI: http://dx.doi.org/10.1080/07036337.2014.9
36. Thomas, L. Jnr and Schwarz, N. D. (2010). 'Wall St. Helped to Mask Debt Fuelling Europe's Crisis. February 13th.
37. Spiegel (2012). 'Chancellor Merkel Vows No Eurobonds as Long as She Lives.' www.spiegel.de › English Site › Europe › Euro Bonds June 27th.
38. Von Weizäcker, J. and Delpla, J. (2010). *The Blue Bond Proposal*, Brueghel Institute Policy Brief, n. 3.

Chapter 6

Regaining the Case

One of the several points made by Yanis Varoufakis from his experience in the Eurogroup of Eurozone finance ministers, and cited earlier, was that the group has no constitutional basis in any Treaty, or written rules of procedure, nor is it accountable to any elected authority. Another, also cited earlier, was was that there was no attempt at dialogue or to recognise the outcome of the January 2015 general election by Wolfgang Schäuble or Jeroen Dijsselbloem, chair of the group. The intent was not only to punish Greece for challenging austerity but to demonstrate to Italy, Spain and Portugal that they also would be so treated.

Yet the electorates in Portugal and Spain nonetheless voted against austerity before the end of the year, while Matteo Renzi of Italy was taking an increasingly intransigent stand against it, and the Commission, and Germany. This chapter considers some of the implications both for them and for France, as well as for actors who have a vested interest in a European recovery including pension funds and sovereign wealth funds, and how the political geometry of Europe may change in the coming year.

Confederalism and the UK Referendum

The issue of immigration has played a key role in the rise of support in Britain for the UK Independence Party (UKIP) which gained three and a half million votes in the 2015 general election. The earlier threat of the mass defection of Conservative voters to UKIP led David Cameron to pledge a referendum on EU membership if elected for a second term. When he won an absolute majority in the 2015 general election this was initially scheduled for 2017 but brought forward to 2016.

When he made plain his negotiating terms in early November 2015, it was improbable that a fundamental change to Britain's position in the EU would be achieved, nor was it indicated as likely by his round of EU heads of state and government. Yet the agreement by the European Council in February 2016 conceded several key points. It explicitly referred to 'enhanced cooperation', of which much has been made in this text in the context of both confederalism and gaining a bond-led investment recovery for the EU, citing that the Treaties contain:

> 'specific conditions whereby some member states are entitled not to take part in or are exempted from the application of certain provisions… as concerns matters such as the adoption of the euro, decisions having defence implications, the exercise of border controls on persons, as well as measures in the areas of freedom, security and justice'.

With reference also to enhanced cooperation, it stated that:

> 'Therefore, such processes make possible different paths of integration for different Member States, allowing those that want to deepen integration to move ahead, whilst respecting the rights of those which do not want to take such a course.'[1]

As Philippe Legrain has commented: 'One big victory for Cameron was that the emergency brake to protect the interests of non-euro members can be pulled by a single government, i.e. Britain alone.[2]

So how come this success? Much because the audience for the message was not only Britain, but also France where the National Front, which had done well in the first round of recent regional elections, was hoping that a Brexit would reinforce political support for a 'Frexit'. Meanwhile, the Polish parliament was about to debate whether or not to leave the Union.[3]

The EU at the time was in disarray on multiple fronts. Notably the failure to deal effectively with the refugee and asylum crisis on which Angela Merkel's leadership was being questioned both outside and within Germany. Her proposal that all member states should agree quotas for refugees had stumbled and the Visegrad 4 of Poland, Hungary, Slovakia and Slovenia had opposed it as a bloc.

In Germany she was being challenged on her refugee policy by Horst Seehofer, leader of her CSU partner in government, and popularity for the CDU-CSU coalition had fallen from 41% in 2015 to 35%. In parallel German public opinion was turning against the EU, with the share of Germans rating the EU positively falling from 45% in May 2015 to 35% in November.[4]

The terrorist attacks in Paris had thrown the border-free Schengen agreement into question. If Schengen failed, border checks between those member states that had agreed it would not only inconvenience individuals, but also slow trade in the internal market. Yet also, austerity was being challenged both by Matteo Renzi in Italy (who in February 2016 compared EU decision-making to the orchestra playing on the decks of the Titanic),[5] and also by electorates in Iberia.

Iberian Challenge 1: Portugal

In Portugal, in 2011, the deflationary eurozone crisis ended six years of government by the Socialist Party and enabled the centre-right Portuguese Social Democrat party – the PSD – led by Pedro Passos Coelho to form a government in coalition with the right-wing Popular Party. The government agreed to a €78 billion European Union bailout and Troika-mandated austerity.

But the Troika austerity conditions pushed the country into its worst recession in forty years. Public sector workers lost between 20 and 30 per cent of their overall income between 2011 and 2014 through a combination of wage cuts, tax increases, longer working hours, reductions in overtime pay, abolished bank holidays and a freeze on promotions. In 2013, unemployment soared to a record 17.5%. Youth unemployment was above 30%. From 2011 some half a million Portuguese emigrated, with nearly a quarter of those remaining in the country below the poverty line.[6]

In the interim there were major anti-austerity rallies and, in 2013, a general strike. Nonetheless, in October 2015, Pedro Passos Coelho's PSD, in another Right-of-Centre electoral coalition – Portugal Ahead (Portugal a Frente) – became the largest political group in a general election, but short of a parliamentary majority.

Inversely, the former mayor of Lisbon and leader of the Portuguese Socialist Party, Antonio Costa, had gained agreement of the Left Bloc – Bloco Esquerda – and of the Portuguese Communist Party – PCP – for a programme for government. Together they had a majority of the seats in parliament and advised the President of the Republic, Anibal Cavaco Silva, that if he invited Passos Coelho to form a government they would call a vote of confidence and defeat it, which they did.

Yet on the defeat of the Passos Coelho coalition in the vote of confidence in the Portuguese parliament, Cavaco Silva stalled, declaring 'In 40 years of democracy, Portuguese governments have never been dependent on anti-European and anti-NATO political forces' and claiming that 'This is the worst moment to radically alter the foundations of our democratic regime'.[7]

As the political activist – and poet – Manuel Alegre commented on Cavaco's claim and the negotiations between the parties of the Left: 'You shouldn't forget that the Portuguese Socialists brought Portugal into Europe and reaffirmed Portugal's membership in NATO. These pillars are not and will not be in question in any of the negotiations'. Adding that: 'We see this 'convergence' [of the Left] as something closer to the Roosevelt New Deal'.[8]

Which was not an accident. At a meeting in Coimbra, Portugal, in 2014, when challenged on whether a European recovery was feasible, Antonio Costa replied 'Yes. Yanis Varoufakis and Stuart Holland have shown so in their *Modest Proposal*'.[9] Moreover, Cavaco then did invite Antonio Costa to form a government, which took office on November 26th 2015.[9] While Antonio Costa already, with good reason, had made the case that:

> 'We can't continue to have a Europe governed by finance ministers, we have to have a Europe governed by politicians. It's increasingly important that decisions are centred on the summits of heads of state and government, and less on the technicalities of finance ministers.'[10]

Not least since it is heads of state and government, not finance ministers, who can determine the 'general economic policies' of the Union which the ECB is obliged to support, and of which a New Deal-style economic recovery, through joint EIB and EIF bonds, with the latter recycling global surpluses, should be part.

Iberian Challenge 2: The Spanish Labyrinth

In Spain, in the general election of 20 December 2015 the People's Party led by Mariano Rajoy failed to gain a working majority. The Spanish Workers' Party (PSOE) came second with 22% and Podemos, founded only a year before, and despite earlier having lost support in some opinion polls, came third with 21%. The Centre-Right Ciudadanos came fourth with just under 14% – still wrongly insisting on the need for 'structural reforms' despite the evidence earlier in the year from the IMF that they had no basis in terms of enhancing efficiency.

Though Mariano Rajoy pronounced that he would form a government with Ciudadanos, he lacked a working parliamentary majority. Pedro Sanchez of PSOE declared that he would not support another government led by Rajoy and the People's Party, whereas Pablo Iglesias of Podemos could support PSOE, as could the Communist-led Popular Unity and the Catalan Greens. With Rajoy losing a vote of confidence in the Cortes the outcome in Spain therefore could in principle be similar to that in Portugal, with an anti-austerity coalition government or a minority government backed by parties also opposed to austerity.

Would the ensuing fate be different from that of Syriza in Greece? PSOE was in some disarray, with a challenge to Pedro Sanchez' leadership.[11] Yet, arguably, yes. Greece is the size of a minor German Land. Spain is the fourth largest economy in the Eurozone. Neither Portugal nor Spain currently were subject to Troika conditionality. Markets had responded calmly to the formation of a Socialist-led government in Portugal, in large part because its finance minister Mario Centeno, rightly, wrongly or simply under constraints, had declared that the government would not cancel its debt and would respect its fiscal obligations according to the Stability Treaty.

Bank stocks plummeted on the Madrid bourse as startled investors awoke to the possibility of an anti-austerity Left-wing coalition. Yet this was a knee-jerk reaction, granted that markets need an end to austerity if they are to gain dividends for shareholders. While, in the view of some commentators, there was no imminent danger of a fresh debt crisis as long as the European Central Bank was buying Spanish bonds under quantitative easing. As Ambrose Evans-Pritchard of *The Telegraph* commented on the result:

> 'If a Socialist-Podemos coalition takes charge at the head of a Left alliance, it will not be singing the IMF tune. It would also be foreign policy disaster for German Chancellor Angela Merkel, who has already lost Italy, Greece, and Portugal to the Left.'[12]

At a meeting of the Executive Committee of PSOE at the end of January 2016, Pedro Sanchez held off the challenge to his leadership by putting the case for a pact with Podemos to the party's membership.[13] It also was clear that Pablo Iglesias, leader of Podemos, was familiar with the case of *The Modest Proposal* when he visited Athens and met with both Alexis Tsipras and Yanis Varoufakis after the electoral success of Syriza in January 2015.

The *Modest Proposal* had not died, but was not tried, had been recognised in 2015 by the Spanish publishing house ARPA, which was publishing an abridged and updated version of my *Europe in Question* early in March 2016, with meetings with politicians, trades unions and representatives of civil society in Barcelona and Madrid.[14]

Restoring Plural Institutional Roles

Some key implications of the above also relate to restoring more plural institutional roles, as follows.

- The IMF

'Powerful Europeans' persuaded Dominique Strauss-Kahn that the IMF should play only a minor role in the Troika. But there is no institutional basis for reducing the IMF to a minor role in resolution of a Eurozone crisis which is damaging not only for Europe but for the global economy. In September 2015, the US and Canada urged the EU to resolve its internal divisions amid concerns the bloc could impede a global recovery, not least with concerns from the OECD that the euro area 'may have fallen into a persistent stagnation trap' with a 'storm warning' from the World Bank both that slowdown in BRICS economies would jeopardise chances of pick-up in global growth in 2016, and that this could be heightened by severe financial market stress.[15]

Moreover, the US in June 2015 had urged both the EU, on the one hand, and the IMF, on the other, to agree a recovery programme to keep Greece in the Eurozone. This would also depend on the willingness of individual governments and central banks to accept a bilateral offer from the IMF. Such as apparently was made to the Central Bank of Greece shortly after the outbreak of the Eurozone crisis and the risk of a Grexit, yet which was rejected by its governor, Yannis Stournaras.[16]

- The ECB

There also is the question of the autonomy of the ECB. As stressed earlier, this is relative inasmuch as, without prejudice to its prior responsibility to preserve the internal and external value of the euro, it has to support the general economic policies of the Union, as defined by heads of state and government. But not to support unilateral policies demanded by only one government or one finance minister or one central bank. Whereas, since Jörg Asmussen's resignation as German executive director, his replacement Sabine Lautenschläger has challenged Mario Draghi on outright monetary easing.

Yet, as Austrian National Bank governor Ewald Nowotny has stressed, the ECB has the responsibility to defend both the *internal* as well as external stability of the euro,[17] and its internal rather than external stability now is in question. Moreover, there is scope for the ECB buying EIB bonds on the secondary market rather than directly, which is one of the recommendations of *The Modest Proposal* which it can and should do without breaching its statutory remit.

- The EIB Group

There also is the major potential of the EIB Group which includes the EIB itself, and the European Investment Fund – EIF – that I designed and Delors persuaded the European Council to establish.

As cited earlier, Jerome Vignon, former deputy head of the President of the Commission's Forward Planning Unit, observed in 2014 that the 'rich legacy' of the Delors 1993 White Paper on *Growth, Competitiveness, Employment*, has gone by default. In particular, through neglect of the creation and wide-ranging terms of reference of the European Investment Fund (EIF).[18]

This has been a main theme of what has gone before, as also that the case for an entirely new European Fund for Strategic Investments (EFSI) – now also part of the EIB Group – was grounded on a reading of the website of the EIF rather than of its statutes and, thereby, a failure to recognise that an EFSI was not needed.

Besides which, since being reduced to a PFI private finance initiative, as recognised by the EIB itself, the EFSI is *demand* based when there is no significant growth in EU demand due to austerity policies.[19] Whereas the rationales for both the EIB and the EIF are *supply* based, but complementary and different in that the design for the EIF was that, unlike the EIB, it should counter the deflationary effects of the debt and debt conditions of the Treaty of Maastricht.[20] This role should be restored in regaining the case for recovery of the EU economies.

Political Geometry

A presidential candidate, François Hollande supported a bond-backed recovery with reference to the case that I had made to Delors. In 2012 he warned that Franco-German cooperation could stall over deep differences on how to resolve the euro crisis, insisting on a climbdown by Angela Merkel in her emphasis on austerity and the surrender of national powers to tighten fiscal discipline. In September 2013, he declared that he did not believe in waiting for a United States of Europe before resolving the Eurozone crisis. In August 2014, he again was calling for economic recovery.[21]

In May 2011, I emailed the then head of research at the SPD, Achim Post, since a member of the Bundestag, with the case that the US New Deal had been the model for the EU bonds in the Delors White Paper. Also that EIB borrowing did not count on national debt nor needed fiscal transfers nor national guarantees and that the EIF could issue recovery bonds within the terms of reference of its own statutes without a Treaty revision.

The feedback was encouraging. He claimed that the case was so strong that he would not simply pass it, as I had requested, to Sigmar Gabriel, later Federal Vice Chancellor, Frank-Walter Steinmeier, later Foreign Minister, or Peer Steinbrück, former finance minister and leader of the SPD's parliamentary group, but recommend a joint meeting with them and their advisers to address it, which he did.

In August 2011 Sigmar Gabriel then criticised the 'failed Eurozone crisis management' of the Merkel government for assuming that the problems have been caused by a lack of fiscal discipline by other member states, and argued that only common liability by governments for Eurozone debt could eliminate instability in financial markets. In April 2012 the three SPD leaders then made a statement on *Why We Need a Social*

Market, in which they said that more national debt and credits were the 'wrong road' but that an investment-led recovery could be achieved through the European Investment Bank and by better use of the Commission's Structural Funds.[22]

Yet there initially was opposition from German Greens.[23] The Greens were against bonds for recovery because they were against growth. It was only later, when Rui Tavares, then in the European Parliament, persuaded key German figures in the Greens in the EP to meet Yanis Varoufakis and myself, that they relented when we had made the case that 'greening' Europe needed not only policies to take out carbon but also investment in green technologies, and that these could not wait indefinitely for a European carbon tax, or a financial transaction tax, as they otherwise had proposed, but needed bond funding.

Moreover, François Hollande's economic adviser, Emmanuel Macron, on becoming Industry Minister had grasped the case – displaced by the European Commission – that joint EIB-EIF bonds could attract global surpluses from sovereign wealth funds.

While also, anti-austerity governments in Spain as well as Portugal could potentially gain support in 2016 from Italy. Thus, in 2014, Matteo Renzi had already led a Centre-Left drive to loosen Eurozone fiscal rules. In 2015, exasperated, he declared that if Brussels were to ask for modifications to the 2016 Italian budget he would send it back unchanged.

After the December election result in Spain, Renzi also blamed austerity for the outcome, declaring that: 'Those who have been in the front line of being the faithful allies of the politics of rigour without growth have lost their jobs'. While also criticising German hegemony in Europe saying, 'I have esteem for Angela Merkel. We have an excellent personal relationship … But we have to be frank … Europe has to serve all 28 countries, not just one'.[24]

Besides which, there is the open question of Poland and whether it would support a bond-backed European recovery programme as had been the aim of its former finance minister Mateusz Szczurek. Clearly, the Law and Justice (PiS) government elected in 2015 is highly controversial. Sacking members of the Constitutional Court, politicising the appointment of prosecutors, and bringing public broadcasting under direct government control has given rise to both major internal and Commission protests. Yet, as Neal Ascherson has commented:

> 'In western Europe, onlookers hear snatches of Law and Justice rhetoric and conclude that the party can be dismissed as "fascist". It is not. It stands for an old-fashioned authoritarian nationalism, invoking traditional Catholic values (imprudently, some in the Catholic hierarchy lend PiS support). And, strangely for westerners, this frantically rightwing party is also the party of what remains of the welfare state, standing up for those millions for whom the transition to capitalism has brought only loss and bewilderment'.[25]

Getting it Clear

If initiated by Italy, with support in 2016 by anti-austerity governments in Spain and Portugal, and giving François Hollande the occasion to join them, a proposal for an EIB-EIF bond-backed investment recovery could, in principle, gain support from the UK, granted that George Osborne declared in July 2011 that he would support Eurobonds for recovery of the EU since this was vital for British exports. There also is potential support from Austria, where chancellor Werner Fayman is more open to the recovery case than Angela Merkel.

But this implies:

1. Distinguishing the private finance initiative premises of a

European Fund for Strategic Investments from bond-funded recovery through the European Investment Bank and the European Investment Fund.

2. Highlighting the New Deal analogy which was the basis for the creation of the European Investment Fund, yet displaced by the Commission in setting up a European Fund for Strategic Investments.

3. Shifting the case for recovery from the Eurogroup of Eurozone finance ministers, to the European Council, as has been recommended by Antonio Costa.

4. Clarifying in Washington – both to the administration and the IMF since both are concerned that there should be a European recovery – that this needs no new institutions or Treaty revisions. Also, vitally, that EIB bonds and on-lending do not count on national debt, which was not known to the no. 2 representative of the IMF to the EU in December 2014.

Mobilising Latent Synergies

Also synergising the case for a bond-backed recovery with those institutions which have a vested interest in it, including employers' federations, pension funds and sovereign wealth funds, as well as rating agencies. This is consistent with the case made by Yanis Varoufakis in relation to our *Modest Proposal* in a statement in Zagreb in May 2013. As he put it:

> 'When addressing diverse audiences ranging from radical activists to hedge fund managers, the idea is to forge strategic alliances even with right-wingers with whom we share a simple interest: an interest to end the negative feedback loop between austerity and crisis, between bankrupt states and bankrupt banks; a negative feedback effect that undermines both capitalism and any progressive programme for replacing it.'[26]

- With Rating Agencies

That such synergies should include rating agenies may appear counter-intuitive. Yet while they can downgrade 'sovereign' debt they cannot themselves govern. Thus, it has been widely overlooked that when Standard & Poor downgraded twelve Eurozone member states' debt in January 2012 it stressed that key reasons were simultaneous debt and spending reductions by governments and households, the weakening thereby of economic growth, and the transparent inability of European policymakers to agree what to do about it.[27]

- With Pension Funds

Similarly, Bill Gross when heading PIMCO, one of the world's largest pension funds with assets of over $1 trillion, also called for European recovery, stressing that pension funds needed growth to secure retirement incomes, whereas low to near zero interest rates in Europe would not enable a fund such as PIMCO to fund retirement incomes.

- With Sovereign Wealth Funds

As also cited earlier, sovereign wealth funds have been damaged by the failure of Europe to gain an economic recovery. Thus, in March 2012 the Norwegian minister of finance announced that Norway's sovereign wealth fund, the world's biggest and hitherto Europe's major institutional investor, would reduce its European commitments from over half to two fifths while raising investments in emerging markets and Asia-Pacific from just over a tenth to two fifths. Yet, since, growth in China has been slowing down. Which increases the need for sovereign wealth funds to find investment outlets in Europe.

- With Trades Unions and Employers' Federations

Synergies also are needed between anti-austerity governments and trades unions, but also with employers' federations: not least since the Economic and Social Committee's 2012 *Restarting Growth* report not only was unanimously endorsed by German employers' representatives, but also by all European employers' representatives on the committee, including Philippe de Beck, president of the European employers' federation *Business Europe*.

- By Enhanced Cooperation

While there also is the option for governments in favour of a joint EIB-EIF-EFSI recovery programme to indicate that, if there is not unanimity for this on the European Council, they could propose it by an 'enhanced cooperation' procedure. Any member state can invoke a qualified majority vote on the procedure. But if invoked by France, Italy, Spain, and with support from others – not excluding the UK, granted George Osborne declaring in 2011 that he would support Eurobonds for recovery of the EU since this was vital for British exports – this could be carried.

Or it may not need to be invoked, rather than made evident as an option. There are two main reasons, both of which should be evident to Angela Merkel. First, that she could not oppose an enhanced cooperation procedure in principle, since Germany had invoked it to outflank David Cameron on a Financial Transaction Tax. Second, that if it were invoked by other member states for an investment-led recovery, Germany could risk being outvoted.

Yet, inversely, she could welcome an indication that other leading member states might move such a procedure if there were not unanimity on a joint EIB-EIF-EFSI recovery programme. There are also three main reasons for this.

First, that it could reconcile her with France and Italy, both of whom were founding member states of the postwar European project. Second, that it would demonstrate that she has no desire for *de facto* German hegemony in the Eurozone that has given rise to protests not only from France and Italy but also from Germans such as Helmut Schmidt, Oskar Lafontaine and Joschka Fischer. Third, that Germany herself, though powerful, cannot assure her own full employment if there is not a recovery of the European economy, not least since her earlier export-led growth in large part had been dependent on exports to China, where demand for them is slowing.

- Multipliers from a Social Investment-Led Recovery

One of the central *Gestalt* shifts needed for this is to reverse the dominant perception that recovery of the European economy depends on restoring private sector confidence. This had been low to negative in the US for the years following the financial crisis of 1929, until the Roosevelt New Deal, and has been the case now for nine years since the onset of the Eurozone crisis. What is needed is a social and green investment-led recovery which can generate multipliers in the private sector.

- With New Deal Legitimation

Yet governments opposed to austerity need to give credible legitimation for alternatives to it and be able to communicate this to, and convince, European electorates in a few words transcending both anti-austerity protests and debates between the cognoscenti on the relative merits, and potential complementarity, of a European Investment Bank or a European Investment Fund and a European Fund for Strategic Investments.

Which now could be the case in a high profile demand in the European Council for *A European New Deal*, while recognising – unlike the parallel NewDeal4Europe proposal,[28] that this does not need fiscal federalism. Also, in making the case for such a New Deal, drawing on the legitimation of its success in the US in the 1930s that encouraged both Harry Truman and the US Congress to endorse the Marshall Plan, which enabled the recovery not only of the postwar German economy but also, thereby, the recovery of German democracy.

The Democracy in Europe Movement

In Berlin in February 2016 Yanis Varoufakis, with others, launched the DiEM25 Democracy in Europe Movement 2025.[29] This is vastly ambitious.

Within 12 months DiEM25 wants full transparency in decision-making: EU Council, Ecofin, and Eurogroup meetings to be live-streamed; minutes of European Central Bank governing council meetings to be published shortly after the meetings have taken place; all documents pertinent to crucial negotiations (e.g. trade-TTIP, 'bailout' loans, Britain's status) to be uploaded on the web; a compulsory register for lobbyists that includes their clients' names, their remuneration, and a record of meetings with officials (both elected and unelected).

Also, within 12 months, to address the on-going economic crisis, utilising existing institutions to resolve four realms: public debt, banking, inadequate investment and rising poverty. At the February 2016 meeting in Berlin, on Yanis' invitation, I presented the case for this including a European New Deal but also for accounting and accountability of major banks and financial institutions previously deemed 'too big to fail'.

Within two years DiEM wants a Constitutional Assembly of representatives elected by at least 15 European countries, with ambitions as wide reaching as those of the Constituent Assembly of the French Revolution. Whether such an Assembly can be achieved remains to be seen. Perhaps so. Yet there is a parallel in this regard with the Conventions and mass protests of the European Nuclear Disarmament – END – campaign, as outlined below.

Further, if vastly ambitious, such a movement also is needed for the tens of millions in Europe who are disillusioned with mainstream politics since they either are unemployed, under-employed, on part-time insecure 'zero hour' contracts, or suffering despair for themselves or for their children.

The European Nuclear Disarmament Precedent

If democratisation of the European Union is not achieved, it may mean its end. The combination of German arrogance and Commission incompetence may finish it on the rising tide of nationalism that spawns on unemployment.

Yet there are precedents for contesting such authoritarianism and incompetence. An example relevant to the DiEM25 agenda was the campaign for European Nuclear Disarmament, (END). Conceived and then mobilised across Europe principally by Ken Coates, of the Bertrand Russell Peace Foundation, its Appeal and its Conventions attracted tens of thousands of supporters while its demonstrations mobilised hundreds of thousands across Europe in opposition to Cruise and Pershing medium range missiles and Soviet SS20s.

END differed from the British CND Campaign for Nuclear Disarmament in not only protesting against nuclear weapons, but in stressing the need for Europe as a non-nuclear security zone. Much as the DiEM25 Democracy in Europe Movement agenda is not only to protest against austerity, but also demonstrate the feasibility of alternatives to it.

END was supported by a range of leading European politicians including, notably, Willy Brandt and Bruno Kreisky, as well as Neil Kinnock. With Robin Cook, I was a member of its executive committee, and drew on it in making this case to the Soviet leadership before Neil's first visit to Moscow as leader of the Labour Party, gaining their agreement to a joint declaration that if a Labour government insisted that the US withdraw Cruise, they would not target Britain with SS20s and would agree to joint site inspection to confirm this.

The Soviets initially were sceptical of END since Edward Thompson, another member of the END executive committee, had linked it with his 'exterminism' thesis which they regarded as anti-Soviet. But, after intensive discussion, they accepted the feasibility of Europe as a zone without medium range missiles since withdrawal of Cruise also was supported by the SPD at a time when Cruise missiles were deployed only in the UK, Germany and Italy.

Within which there was a credible political and security logic. If the governments of two of these three countries would insist on their withdrawal the third would be most likely to do so since it would not welcome being the only target for Soviet SS20s. Through its combination of a mass protest movement, and political support, END influenced the context, and credibility for the Soviets, of the 1987 INF Treaty on intermediate nuclear forces, which was the only one to successfully outlaw a whole class of missiles (Cruise, Pershing and SS20s).

Notes

1. European Council (2016). Decision of the Heads of State or Government, Meeting within the European Council, Concerning a New Settlement for the United Kingdom within the European Union. EUCO 1/16. Brussels, 1 February.
2. Legrain, P. (2016). http://capx.co/thanks-to-david-camerons-deal-britain-has-the-best-of-both-worlds/ February 20th.
3. Chassany, A-S. (2016). French far-right hopes Brexit will inspire Frexit. The Financial Times. February 18th.
4. Wagstyl, S. (2016).' An open door to new friends.' The Financial Times. February 17th.
5. Bloomberg (2016). 'Renzi Says EU Can Dodge Titanic Disaster Following Italy's Lead.' February 11th.
6. Wise, P. (2015). 'Portugal divided by austerity.' The Financial Times. December 1st
7. ZAP (2015). Cavaco estuda 'Governo de Transição'. November 19th
8. Redmont, D. (2015). 'The old fights of Lisbon's new left: Portugal's left-wing politicians cut their teeth as militants against the Salazar regime.' Politico. November 22nd. www.politico.eu/article/the-old-fights-of-lisbons-new-left
9. Report by Manuel Porto, former Dean of the Law Faculty of the University of Coimbra on speech by Antonio Costa at Quinta das Lagrimas, Coimbra.
10. Reuters (2015). 'Portugal president tells Socialists not to compromise on cuts with far left.' November 23rd.
11. Buck, T. (2016). 'Socialist rebellion threatens Sanchez the kingmaker.' The Financial Times. January 2nd-3rd.
12. Evans-Pritchard, A. (2015). 'Political uprising in Spain shatters illusion of eurozone recovery.' The Telegraph. December 21st
13. Directory (2016). 'Sanchez agrees to consult PSOE membership on a possible pact for .' January 30th.
14. Holland, S. (2016). *Contra la Hegemonia de la Austeridade – Alternativas para l'Europa.* Barcelona: Arpa Editores.
15. www.ft.com/…/4137a208-4160-11e4-b98f-00144fe… www.oecd.org/eco/outlook/economicoutlook.htm
16. Varoufakis to myself shortly after he became finance minister. I

had met with Yannis Stournaras when he earlier had been Governor of the National Bank of Greece and was able to clarify to him that EIB lending did not count on Greek national debt, which he did not know. Before becoming Governor of the Bank of Greece he also was Greek finance minister.
17. Opening remarks by Professor Dr. Ewald Nowotny, Governor of the National Bank of the Republic of Austria, at the 41st Economics Conference of the Bank. Vienna. June 2013. Op. cit.
18. Vignon, J. (2014). The Rich Legacy of the White Paper on Growth, Competitiveness and Employment. Op. cit.
19. http://www.eib.org/about/invest-eu/index.htm?media=shortlink
20. Holland, S. (1993). *The European Imperative: Economic and Social Cohesion* (Foreword Jacques Delors). Nottingham: Spokesman Books.
21. Chrisafis, A. and Traynor, I. (2012). 'Hollande fires warning shot at Merkel over austerity on eve of EU summit.' The Guardian, October 17th.
    Cazenave, F. (2013). 'Hollande ne croit pas aux Etats-Unis d'Europe.' Le Taurillon. September 13th.
    EU Observer (2014). 'Hollande calls for recovery.' news-twice-daily@list.euobserver.com, August 5th.
22. Deutschlandfunk (2008). Gabriel: Müssen ein gemeinsames Investitionsprogramm anschieben. *Bundesumweltminister fordert europäischen 'New Deal' für Arbeit und Umwelt* November 5th.
    SPD (2012) Großer Europa-Appell der SPD-Troika. Warum wir die Soziale Marktwirtschaft brauchen. April 1st
23. Die Welt (2012). 'Rot-Grün distanziert sich von Hollandes Euro-Bonds.' May 24th.
24. The Financial Times (2014). 'Renzi leads centre-left drive to loosen eurozone fiscal rules.' www.ft.com June 19th
    Politi, J. (2015). 'Brussels warns Italy over violating EU budget rules.' The Financial Times. November 17th
    Renzi blames austerity for boosting populism and warns the EU must serve 'all 28 countries not just one.' The Financial Times. December 22nd.
25. Ascherson, N. (2016). The assault on democracy in Poland is dangerous for the Poles and all Europe. The Guardian. January 17th.
26. Varoufakis, Y. (2013). Confessions of an Erratic Marxist.

Conference Address Zagreb.
27. The Telegraph (2012). 'Standard & Poor's cuts ratings of nine Eurozone countries.' Op. cit.
28. NewDeal4Europe, Op. Cit.
29. DiEM25. (2016). Democracy in Europe Movement. Manifesto. Berlin. February 9th

Annex
A Modest Proposal for Resolving the Eurozone Crisis.

Yanis Varoufakis, Stuart Holland and James K. Galbraith

Prologue

Europe is fragmenting. While the European Central Bank has managed to stabilise bond markets, the economies of the European core and its periphery are drifting apart. As this happens, human costs mount and disintegration becomes an increasing threat.

But this is not just a matter for the Eurozone. The fallout from a Eurozone breakup poses a global danger.

Following a sequence of errors and avoidable delays Europe's leadership remains in denial about the nature of the crisis, and continues to pose the false choice between draconian austerity and a federal Europe.

By contrast, we propose immediate solutions, feasible within current European law and treaties.

There are, in this crisis, four sub-crises: a banking crisis, a public debt crisis, a crisis of under-investment, and now a social crisis – the result of five years of policy failure. Our Modest Proposal therefore now has four elements. They deploy existing institutions and require none of the moves that many Europeans oppose, such as national guarantees or fiscal transfers. Nor do they require treaty changes, which many electorates anyway could reject. Thus we propose a European New Deal which, like its American forebear, would lead to progress within months, yet through measures that fall entirely within the constitutional framework to which European governments have already agreed.

Four Crises

The Eurozone crisis is unfolding on four interrelated domains.

Banking crisis: There is a common global banking crisis, which was sparked off mainly by the catastrophe in American finance. But the Eurozone has proved uniquely unable to cope with the disaster, and this is a problem of structure and governance. The Eurozone features a central bank with no government, and national governments with no supportive central bank, arrayed against a global network of mega-banks they cannot possibly supervise. Europe's response has been to propose a full Banking Union – a bold measure in principle but one that threatens both delay and diversion from actions that are needed immediately.

Debt crisis: The credit crunch of 2008 revealed the Eurozone's principle of perfectly separable public debts to be unworkable. Forced to create a bailout fund that did not violate the no-bailout clauses of the ECB charter and Lisbon Treaty, Europe created the temporary European Financial Stability Facility (EFSF) and then the permanent European Stability Mechanism (ESM). The creation of these new institutions met the immediate funding needs of several member states, but retained the flawed principle of separable public debts and so could not contain the crisis. One sovereign state, Cyprus, has now de facto gone bankrupt, imposing capital controls even while remaining inside the euro.

During the summer of 2012, the ECB came up with another approach: the Outright Monetary Transactions programme (OMT). OMT succeeded in calming the bond markets for a while. But it too fails as a solution to the crisis, because it is based on a threat against bond markets that cannot remain credible over time. And while it puts the public debt crisis on hold, it fails to reverse it; ECB bond purchases cannot restore the lending power of failed markets or the borrowing power of failing governments.

Investment crisis: Lack of investment in Europe threatens its living standards and its international competitiveness. As Germany alone ran large surpluses after 2000, the resulting trade imbalances ensured that when crisis hit in 2008, the deficit zones would collapse. And the burden of adjustment fell exactly on the deficit zones, which could not bear it. Nor could it be offset by devaluation or new public spending, so the scene was set for disinvestment in the regions that needed investment the most.

Thus, Europe ended up with both low total investment and an even more uneven distribution of that investment between its surplus and deficit regions.

Social crisis: Three years of harsh austerity have taken their toll on Europe's peoples. From Athens to Dublin and from Lisbon to Eastern Germany, millions of Europeans have lost access to basic goods and dignity. Unemployment is rampant. Homelessness and hunger are rising. Pensions have been cut; taxes on necessities meanwhile continue to rise. For the first time in two generations, Europeans are questioning the European project, while nationalism, and even Nazi parties, are gaining strength.

Four Political Constraints

Any solution to the crisis must respect realistic constraints on political action. This is why grand schemes should be shunned. It is why we need a modest proposal.

Four constraints facing Europe presently are that:

(a) the ECB will not be allowed to monetise sovereigns directly. There will be no ECB guarantees of debt issues by member states, no ECB purchases of government bonds in the primary market, no ECB leveraging to buy sovereign debt from either the primary or secondary markets.

(b) the ECB's outright monetary easing OMT programme has been tolerated insofar as no bonds are actually purchased. OMT is a policy that does not match stability with growth and, sooner or later, will be found wanting.

(c) surplus countries will not consent to 'jointly and severally' guaranteed Eurobonds to mutualise debt, and deficit countries will resist the loss of sovereignty that would be demanded of them without a properly functioning federal transfer union which Germany, understandably, rejects.

(d) Europe cannot wait for federation. If crisis resolution is made to depend on federation, the Eurozone will fail first. The treaty changes necessary to create a proper European Treasury, with the powers to tax, spend and borrow, cannot, and must not, be held to precede resolution of this crisis.

The next section presents four policies that recognise these constraints.

Four Alternative Policies

The Modest Proposal introduces no new EU institutions and violates no existing treaty. Instead, we propose that existing institutions be used in ways that remain within the letter of European legislation but allow for new functions and policies.

These institutions are:

> The European Central Bank – ECB
> The European Investment Bank – EIB
> The European Investment Fund – EIF
> The European Stability Mechanism – ESM

Policy 1: A Case-by-Case Bank Programme

For the time being, we propose that banks in need of recapitalisation from the ESM be turned over to the ESM directly – instead of having the national government borrow on the bank's behalf. Banks from Cyprus, Greece and Spain would likely fall under this proposal. The ESM, and not the national government, would then restructure, recapitalise and resolve the failing banks, dedicating the bulk of its funding capacity to this purpose.

The Eurozone must eventually become a single banking area with a single banking authority. But this final goal has become the enemy of good current policy. At the June 2012 European Summit direct bank recapitalisation was agreed upon in principle, but was made conditional on the formation of a Banking Union. Since then, the difficulties of legislating, designing and implementing a Banking Union have meant delay and dithering. A year after that sensible decision, the deadly embrace between insolvent national banking systems and insolvent member states continues.

Today the dominant EU view remains that a Banking Union must be completed before the ESM directly recapitalises banks. And that, when it is complete, the ESM's contribution will be partial and come only after a bail-in of depositors in the fiscally-stressed countries of the periphery. That way, the banking crisis will either never be resolved or its resolution will be delayed for years, risking a new financial implosion.

Our proposal is that a national government should have the option of waiving its right to supervise and resolve a failing bank. Shares equivalent to the needed capital injection will then pass to the ESM, and the ECB and ESM will appoint a new Board of Directors. The new board will conduct a full review of the bank's position and will recommend to the ECB-ESM a course for reform of the bank.

Reform may entail a merger, downsizing, even a full resolution of the bank, with the understanding that steps will be taken to avoid, above all, a haircut of deposits. Once the bank has been restructured and recapitalised, the ESM will sell its shares and recoup its costs.

The above proposal can be implemented today, without a Banking Union or any treaty changes. The experience that the ECB and the ESM will acquire from this case-by-case process will help hone the formation of a proper Banking Union once the present crisis recedes.

Policy 2: A Limited Debt Conversion Programme

The Maastricht Treaty permits each European member state to issue sovereign debt up to 60% of GDP. Since the crisis of 2008, most Eurozone member states have exceeded this limit. We propose that the ECB offer member states the opportunity of a debt conversion for their Maastricht Compliant Debt (MCD), while the national shares of the converted debt would continue to be serviced separately by each member state.

The ECB, faithful to the non-monetisation constraint (a) above, would not seek to buy or guarantee sovereign MCD debt directly or indirectly. Instead it would act as a go-between, mediating between investors and member states. In effect, the ECB would orchestrate a conversion-servicing loan for the MCD, for the purposes of redeeming those bonds upon maturity.

The conversion servicing loan works as follows. Refinancing of the Maastricht-compliant share of the debt, now held in ECB-bonds, would be by member states but at interest rates set by the ECB just above its bond yields. The shares of national debt converted to ECB-bonds are to be held by it in debit accounts. These cannot be used as collateral for credit or derivatives creation. Member states will undertake to redeem bonds in full on maturity, if the holders opt for this rather than to extend them at lower, more secure rates offered by the ECB.

Governments that wish to participate in the scheme can do so on the basis of Enhanced Cooperation, which needs at least nine member states. Those not opting in can keep their own bonds even for their Maastricht Compliant Debt. To safeguard the credibility of this conversion, and to provide a backstop for the ECB-bonds that requires no ECB monetisation, member states agree to afford their ECB debit accounts super-seniority status, and the ECB's conversion-servicing loan mechanism may be insured by the ESM, utilising only a small portion of the latter's borrowing capacity. If a member state goes into a disorderly default before an ECB-bond issued on its behalf matures, then that ECB-bond payment will be covered by insurance purchased or provided by the ESM.

Why not continue with the ECB's Outright Monetary Transactions programme?

The ECB has succeeded in taming interest rate spreads within the Eurozone by announcing its Outright Monetary Transactions programme (OMT). OMT was conceived as unlimited support of stressed Euro-Area bonds – Italy's and Spain's in particular – so as to end the contagion and save the euro from collapse.

However, political and institutional pressures meant that the threat against bond dealers, which was implicit in the OMT announcement, had to be diluted to a conditional programme. The conditionality involves troika-supervision over the governments to be helped by the OMT, who are obliged to sign a draconian memorandum of understanding before OMT takes effect. The problem is not only that this of itself does nothing to address the need for both stability and growth, but that the governments of Spain and Italy would not survive signing such a memorandum of understanding, and therefore have not done so.

Thus OMT's success in quelling the bond markets is based on a non-credible threat. So far, not one bond has been purchased. This constitutes an open invitation to bond dealers to test the ECB's resolve at a time of their choosing. It is a temporary fix bound to stop working when circumstances embolden the bond dealers. That may happen when volatility returns to global bond markets once the Federal Reserve and the Bank of Japan begin to curtail their quantitative easing programmes.

Policy 3: An Investment-led Recovery and Convergence Programme

In principle the EU already has a recovery and convergence strategy in the European Economic Recovery Programme 2020. In practice this has been shredded by austerity. We propose that the European Union launch a new investment programme to reverse the recession, strengthen European integration, restore private sector confidence and fulfil the commitment of the Rome Treaty to raising standards of living, and that of the 1986 Single European Act to economic and social cohesion.

The Investment-led Recovery and Convergence Programme (IRCP) will be co-financed by bonds issued jointly by the European Investment Bank (EIB) and the European Investment Fund (EIF). The EIB has a remit to invest in health, education, urban renewal, urban environment, green technology and green power generation, while the EIF both can co-finance EIB investment projects and should finance a European Venture Capital Fund, which was part of its original design.

A key principle of this proposal is that investment in these social and environmental domains should be europeanised. Borrowing for such investments should not count on national debt any more than US Treasury borrowing counts on the debt of California or Delaware. The under-recognised precedents for this are: (1) that no European member state counts EIB borrowing against national debt, and: (2) that the EIB has successfully issued bonds since 1958 without national guarantees.

EIB-EIF finance of an Investment-led Recovery and Convergence Programme therefore does not need national guarantees or a common fiscal policy. Instead, the joint bonds can be serviced directly by the revenue streams of the EIB-EIF-funded investment projects. This can be carried out within member states and will not need fiscal transfers between them.

A European Venture Capital Fund financed by EIF bonds was backed unanimously by employers and trades unions on the Economic and Social Committee in their 2012 report *Restarting Growth*. Central European economies (Germany and Austria) already have excellent finance for small and medium firms through their *Mittelstandspolitik*. It is the peripheral economies that need this, to build new sectors, to foster convergence and cohesion and to address the growing imbalances of competitiveness within the Eurozone.

Rationale

The transmission mechanism of monetary policy to the periphery of Europe has broken down. Mr Mario Draghi admits this. He has gone on record to suggest that the EIB play an active role in restoring investment financing in the periphery. Mr Draghi is right on this point.

But, for the Investment-led Recovery and Convergence

Programme (IRCP) to reverse the Eurozone recession and stop the de-coupling of the core from the periphery, it must be large enough to have a significant effect on the GDP of the peripheral countries.

If EIB-EIF bonds are to be issued on this scale, some fear that their yields may rise. But this is far from clear. The world is awash in savings seeking sound investment outlets. Issues of EIF bonds that co-finance EIB investment projects should meet these demands, supporting stability and working to restore growth in the European periphery.

We therefore submit that joint EIB-EIF bond issues can succeed without formal guarantees. Nonetheless, in fulfilment of its remit to support 'the general economic policies in the Union', the ECB can issue an advance or precautionary statement that it will partially support EIB-EIF bonds by means of standard central bank refinancing or secondary market operations. Such a statement should suffice to allow the EIB-EIF funded IRCP to be large enough for the purposes of bringing about Europe's recovery.

Misleading arguments and unworkable alternatives:

There are calls for bonds to finance infrastructure, neglecting the fact that this has been happening through the European Investment Bank (EIB) for more than half a century. An example is a recent European Commission proposal for 'Project Bonds' to be guaranteed by member states. This assures opposition from many of them, not least Germany, while ignoring the fact that the EIB has issued project bonds successfully since 1958, without such guarantees.

There is no high-profile awareness that EIB investment finance does not count on national debt.

There is a widespread presumption that public investment drains the private sector when in fact it sustains and supports it. There is similar presumption that one cannot solve the crisis by 'piling debt on debt'. It depends on which debt for which purpose, and at what rates. Piling up national debt at interest rates of up to seven per cent or more without recovery is suicidal. Funding inflows from global surpluses to Europe to promote economic recovery through joint EIB-EIF bonds at interest rates which could be less than two per cent is entirely sustainable.

There is little awareness of the EIB's sister organisation, the European Investment Fund (EIF), which has a large potential for investment funding of SMEs, high technology clusters and a variety of other projects, which it can co-finance with bonds, issued jointly with the EIB.

Why aren't the EIB-EIF doing this now?

Until the onset of the Eurozone crisis the EIB had succeeded in gaining national co-finance, or co-finance from national institutions, for its investments. But with the crisis this annual co-finance fell from over €82 billion in 2008 to only €45 billion in 2012. The EIF is a sister institution of the EIB within the EIB Group. EIF bonds issued from now could match EIB bonds without a treaty revision or an amendment of EIF statutes. Like EIB bonds, EIF bonds need not count on national debt or need national guarantees. The EIB would retain control over project approval and monitoring.

In sum, we recommend that:

The Investment-led Recovery and Cohesion Programme be funded by means of jointly-issued EIB and EIF bonds without any formal guarantees or fiscal transfers by member states.

Both EIB and EIF bonds be redeemed by the revenue stream of the investment projects they fund, as EIB bonds always have been.

If needed, the ECB should stand by to assist in keeping yields low, through direct purchases of EIB-EIF bonds in the secondary market.

Policy 4: An Emergency Social Solidarity Programme

We recommend that Europe embark immediately on an Emergency Social Solidarity Programme (ESSP) that will guarantee access to nutrition and to basic energy needs for all Europeans, by means of a European Food Stamp Programme modelled on its US equivalent and a European Minimum Energy Programme.

These programmes would be funded by the European Commission using the interest accumulated within the European system of central banks, from TARGET 2 imbalances, profits made from government bond transactions and, in the future, other financial transactions or balance sheet stamp duties that the EU is currently considering.

Rationale

Europe now faces the worst human and social crisis since the late 1940s. In member states like Greece, Ireland, Portugal, but also elsewhere in the Eurozone, including core countries, basic needs are not being met. This is true especially for the elderly, the unemployed, for young children, for children in schools, for the disabled, and for the homeless.

There is a plain moral imperative to act to satisfy these needs. In addition, Europe faces a clear and present danger from extremism, racism, xenophobia and even outright Nazism –

notably in countries like Greece that have borne the brunt of the crisis. Never before have so many Europeans held the European Union and its institutions in such low esteem. The human and social crisis is turning quickly into a question of legitimacy for the European Union.

Reason for TARGET 2 funding

TARGET 2 is a technical name for the system of internal accounting of monetary flows between the central banks that make up the European System of Central Banks. In a well-balanced Eurozone, where the trade deficit of a member state is financed by a net flow of capital to that same member state, the liabilities of that state's central bank to the central banks of other states would just equal its assets. Such a balanced flow of trade and capital would yield a TARGET 2 figure near zero for all member states. And that was, more or less, the case throughout the Eurozone before the crisis.

However, the crisis caused major imbalances that were soon reflected in huge TARGET 2 imbalances. As inflows of capital to the periphery dried up, and capital began to flow in the opposite direction, the central banks of the peripheral countries began to amass large net liabilities and the central banks of the surplus countries equally large net assets.

The Eurozone's designers had attempted to build a disincentive within the intra-Eurosystem real-time payments system, so as to prevent the build-up of huge liabilities on one side and corresponding assets on the other. This took the form of charging interest on the net liabilities of each national central bank, at an interest rate equal to the ECB's main refinancing level. These payments are distributed to the central banks of the surplus member states, which then pass them on to their government treasury.

Thus the Eurozone was built on the assumption that TARGET 2 imbalances would be isolated, idiosyncratic events, to be corrected by national policy action. The system did not take account of the possibility that there could be fundamental structural asymmetries and a systemic crisis.

Today, the vast TARGET 2 imbalances are the monetary tracks of the crisis. They trace the path of the consequent human and social disaster hitting mainly the deficit regions. The increased TARGET 2 interest would never have accrued if the crises had not occurred. They accrue only because, for instance, risk-averse Spanish and Greek depositors, reasonably enough, transfer their savings to a Frankfurt bank.

As a result, under the rules of the TARGET 2 system, the central banks of Spain and of Greece have to pay interest to the Bundesbank – to be passed along to the Federal Government in Berlin. This indirect fiscal boost to the surplus country has no rational or moral basis. Yet the funds are there, and could be used to deflect the social and political danger facing Europe.

There is a strong case to be made that the interest collected from the deficit Member states' central banks should be channelled to an account that would fund our proposed Emergency Social Solidarity Programme (ESSP). Additionally, if the EU introduces a financial transactions tax, or stamp duty proportional to the size of corporate balance sheets, a similar case can be made as to why these receipts should fund the ESSP. With this proposal, the ESSP is not funded by fiscal transfers nor national taxes.

Years of crisis have culminated in a Europe that is losing its dynamism in the eyes of the world and its legitimacy in the eyes of Europeans. Europe is unnecessarily back in recession.

While the bond markets were placated by the ECB's actions in the summer of 2012, the Eurozone remains on the road toward disintegration.

False Choices

While this process eats away at Europe's potential for shared prosperity, European governments are imprisoned by false choices:

– between stability and growth;
– between austerity and stimulus;

– between the deadly embrace of insolvent banks by insolvent governments, and an admirable but undefined and indefinitely delayed Banking Union;

– between the principle of perfectly separable country debts and the supposed need to persuade the surplus countries to bankroll the rest;

– between national sovereignty and federalism.

These falsely dyadic choices imprison thinking, and immobilise governments. They are responsible for a legitimation crisis for the European project. And they risk a catastrophic human, social and democratic crisis in Europe.

By contrast the Modest Proposal *counters that:*

The real choice is between beggar-my-neighbour deflation and an investment-led recovery combined with social stabilisation. The investment recovery will be funded by global capital, supplied principally by sovereign wealth funds and by pension funds which are seeking long-term investment outlets. Social stabilisation can be funded, initially, through the Target 2 payments scheme.

Taxpayers in Germany and the other surplus nations do not need to bankroll the 2020 European Economic Recovery Programme, the restructuring of sovereign debt, resolution of the banking crisis, or the emergency humanitarian programme so urgently needed in the European periphery.

Neither an expansionary monetary policy nor a fiscal stimulus in Germany and other surplus countries, though welcome, would be sufficient to bring recovery to Europe.

Treaty changes for a federal union may be aspired to by some, but will take too long, are opposed by many, and are not needed to resolve the crisis now.

On this basis the *Modest Proposal's* four policies are feasible steps by which to deal decisively with Europe's banking crisis, the debt crisis, underinvestment, unemployment as well as the human, social and political emergency.

The Modest Proposal offers immediate answers to questions about the credibility of the ECB's OMT policy, the impasse on a Banking Union, financing of SMEs, green energy and high tech start-ups in Europe's periphery, and basic human needs that the crisis has left untended.

Cutting the Gordian Knot

It is not known how many strokes Alexander the Great needed to cut the Gordian knot. But in four strokes, Europe could cut through the knot of debt and deficits in which it has bound itself.

In one stroke, Policy 1, the Case-by-Case Bank Programme (CCBP), bypasses the impasse of the Banking Union (BU), decoupling stressed sovereign debt from banking recapitalisation, and allowing for a proper BU to be designed at leisure.

By another stroke, Policy 2, the Limited Debt Conversion Programme (LDCP), the Eurozone's mountain of debt shrinks, through an ECB-ESM conversion of Maastricht-Compliant member state Debt.

By a third stroke, Policy 3, the Investment-led Recovery and Convergence Programme (IRCP) recycles global surpluses into European investments.

By a fourth stroke, Policy 4, the Emergency Social Solidarity Programme (ESSP), deploys funds created from the asymmetries that helped cause the crisis, to meet basic human needs caused by the crisis itself.

At the political level, the four policies of the *Modest Proposal* constitute a process of decentralised europeanisation, to be juxtaposed against an authoritarian federation that has not been put to European electorates, is unlikely to be endorsed by them, and, critically, offers them no assurance of higher levels of employment and welfare.

We propose that four areas of economic activity be europeanised: banks in need of ESM capital injections, sovereign debt management, the recycling of European and global savings into socially productive investment and prompt financing of a basic social emergency programme.

Our proposed europeanisation of borrowing for investment retains a large degree of subsidiarity. It is consistent with greater sovereignty for member states than that implied by a federal structure, and it is compatible with the principle of reducing excess national debt once banks, debt and investment flows are europeanised, without the need for national guarantees or fiscal transfers.

While broad in scope, the *Modest Proposal* suggests no new institutions and does not aim at redesigning the Eurozone. It needs no new rules, fiscal compacts, or troikas. It requires no prior agreement to move in a federal direction while allowing for consent through enhanced cooperation rather than imposition of austerity.

It is in this sense that this proposal is, indeed, modest.

Glossary
Relevant Institutions and Decision-Making Procedures

ECB – European Central Bank. Generally assumed to be entirely independent of political influence. But which, without prejudice to its obligation to assure the internal and external stability of the currency, on the lines of the previous terms of reference of the Bundesbank, also is obliged to support 'the general economic policies of the Union' which can be defined by heads of state and government.

EEC – European Economic Community, agreed in March 1957 by Germany, France, Italy and the Benelux countries.

EFTA – The European Free Trade Association, formed in 1960 on the initiative of the UK and including Austria, Denmark, Norway, Portugal, Sweden, Switzerland and the UK. Finland became an associate member in 1961 and a full member in 1986, and Iceland joined in 1970.

EIB – European Investment Bank. The bond issuing non-profit borrowing and lending institution of the European Union, established in 1958 and whose funding does not count on the national debt of EU member states, despite this not being recognised as late as December 2014 by the economic advisers to European Council President Donald Tusk, to Commission President Jean-Claude Juncker, to Commissioner Jyrki Katainen, to the senior economic adviser to the Commission or to the no. 2 representative of the IMF to the European Union.

EIF – A non-profit European Investment Fund now part of the EIB Group and which, like the EIB, can issue bonds that do not count on national debt. Proposed to Jacques Delors in 1993 and established in 1994 to offset the EIB's 'house rule' that it would only finance half of any national or transational

European investment, and to recycle global surpluses.

EFSI – European Fund for Strategic Investments. A Fund established in November 2014 on the misplaced presumption that the European Investment Fund could only offer support for small and medium firms, which had been only a micro dimension of its macroeconomic design. But a Fund only in name since it is a PFI-Private Finance Initiative, unlikely to gain sufficient funding for even a significant infrastructure-led European recovery.

EMV – Enabling Majority Voting. Proposed on the Giscard Commission for a Constitution for Europe by Giuliano Amato. Inverting QMV and by which a majority voting procedure should be put before decision to national parliaments, and which would not bind those member states opposed, thereby safguarding national democracy.

END – The European Nuclear Disarmament campaign. Through its combination of a mass protest movement, and political support, END influenced the context, and credibility for the Soviets, of the 1987 INF Treaty on intermediate nuclear forces which was the only one to successfully outlaw a whole class of missiles.

Enhance Cooperation– A procedure by which a third of Member States can adopt a policy without this binding others. Recognised in the European Council (2016). Decisions of the Heads of State or Government, concerning a new settlement for the United Kingdom within the European Union (EUCO 1/16. Brussels 19 February). Implies confederalism rather than 'ever closer union'.

ESM – Since October 2012 the European Stability Mechanism has been intended to be a crisis resolution mechanism for countries of the euro area. It can issue debt instruments in order to finance loans and other forms of financial assistance to euro member states. But there has been disagreement concerning what it can or should do, including German opposition to its increasing the subscribed capital of the European Investment Fund to back its issue of Eurobonds – proposed by France, with legal backing.

EU – European Union. Renaming the European Community in 1992 at the Treaty of Maastricht and thereby reinforcing the concept of 'ever closer union'. But thereby downgrading the 1986 Single European Act commitment to economic and social cohesion as the basis of a community of member states and societies rather than a federalist project.

European Council – Heads of state and government with the power to define 'general ecconomic policies' which the European Central Bank, without prejudice to its remit to assure the internal and external stability of the currency, is obliged to support. But which, since inflation is now near zero, and the disintegration of the Eurozone through popular reaction against austerity is possible, could enable it to decide that a 'general economic policy' of the EU is a bond-backed economic recovery on the lines of the US New Deal, yet without needing fiscal federalism.

Eurobonds – Fixed interest borrowing. Wrongly presumed by Germany to mean mutualisation of member states' debt. Used in this volume, in line with the recommendation of EU bonds to Jacques Delors in 1993, to mean bonds attracting surpluses from pension funds and sovereign wealth funds to recycle global surpluses without needing guarantees from member states, nor counting on their national debt.

QMV – Qualified majority voting, binding minority

governments, as in the design of Jean Monnet for the European Coal and Steel Community. Yet then blocked in the EEC by De Gaulle in the Luxembourg Compromise of January 1966 on the basis that QMV would not obtain in cases of 'important national interest'. Which also could have been included in a Treaty of Accession for the UK and other EFTA member states after gaining De Gaulle's support in principle for a second British application to join the EEC in 1967.

Endorsements of *Europe in Question* and *The Modest Proposal*

Yanis Varoufakis, University of Athens and formerly Finance Minister of Greece.
Stuart Holland on Europe is akin to Thomas Paine on the French Revolution combined with John Maynard Keynes on The Economic Consequences of the Peace. At a precociously young age, he persuaded Charles De Gaulle to agree to Britain's second application to join the European Economic Community. As an advisor to Jack Delors he designed solutions to Europe's current problems decades before they even surfaced. Now, with *Europe in Question – and what to do about it* he offers a new generation of readers unique insights on how Europe can be fixed – as well as warnings that it may not be.

Giuliano Amato, Former Prime Minister and Finance Minister of Italy
Members of the Juncker Commission may have little time to read books rather than briefings, but should read this one. His high level experience and initiatives on Europe since the 1960s have been exceptional. His case that EIB bonds do not count on national debt nor need fiscal transfers and could recycle global surpluses counterparts the priority being given by Jean-Claude Juncker to an investment-led recovery of the EU.

Antonio Guterres, Former Prime Minister of Portugal and UN High Commissioner for Refugees
His foes are inequality and ideological and political hegemony. His stress that EIB bonds can promote cohesion is backed by the extension of the terms of reference in the Amsterdam Special Action Programme to invest in health, education, urban renewal and safeguarding the environment. His case that the G20 should nominate a World Development Organization to

liaise more effectively with UN institutions and multilateral development banks also is typically innovative.

Michel Rocard, Former Prime Minister of France, in Preface to the French Edition of The Modest Proposal 4.0 by Yanis Varoufakis, Stuart Holland and James Galbraith
I love the title of this *Modest Proposal*. Not least since it neither is modest by ambition nor in intelligence. Its aim is to resolve the Eurozone crisis without directly confronting the sovereignty of any major state, and notably not that of Germany. It combines awareness of room for manoeuvre displaced by monetary authorities for decades and affirms that there can be solutions within existing institutional frameworks.

Europe in Question is available as an eBook on Amazon and as a paperback from Spokesman, Nottingham.

EUROPE IN QUESTION

and what to do about it

by

STUART HOLLAND

Biographical Note

Born in 1940, Stuart Holland studied and taught history and political theory at Oxford, then became an adviser to Harold Wilson on European affairs and gained the consent of Charles De Gaulle for a second British application to join the European Community on the basis of confederal rather than federal decision-making and mutual currency support. Resigning from 10 Downing Street when Wilson did not follow this through, he completed a doctorate in economics and drafted what in the early 1970s became the economic programme of the British Labour Party. From 1979 to 1989 he was a Labour Member of Parliament and shadow minister, before leaving Westminster to help Jacques Delors shape EU policies for economic and social cohesion. His proposals to Delors for Eurobonds to offset the deflationary Maastricht debt and deficit conditions resurfaced during the Eurozone crisis and have attracted attention and support from anti-austerity parties and governments.